English Reading Comprehension

Success in
Year 5

Written and illustrated
by Jim Edmiston

Acknowledgements:

Author: Jim Edmiston
Cover Design: Jim Edmiston and Kathryn Webster

The right of Jim Edmiston to be identified as the author of this publication has been asserted by him in accordance with the Copyright, Designs and Patents Act 1998.

HeadStart Primary Ltd
Elker Lane
Clitheroe
BB7 9HZ

T. 01200 423405
E. info@headstartprimary.com
www.headstartprimary.com

All rights reserved. No part of this publication may be reproduced, stored in a retrieval system, or transmitted in any form or by any means, electronic, mechanical, photocopying, recording or otherwise without the prior permission of the publisher.

Published by HeadStart Primary Ltd 2016 © **HeadStart Primary Ltd 2016**

A record for this book is available from the British Library -
ISBN: 978-1-908767-36-3

Year 5

CONTENTS

Introduction	2
Words in context	3
Explaining words in context	13
Retrieving and recording information	19
Fact and opinion	35
The main idea	41
Summarising main ideas	49
Details that support the main idea	55
Inferences	59
Justifying inferences with evidence	67
Predicting what might happen	73
Features of texts	79
Features of texts and meaning	85
Words that capture the reader's imagination	93
Explaining how words and phrases enhance meaning	101
Themes and conventions	107
Making comparisons	111
List of tests (range of texts)	117
Test A	119
Answers and mark scheme – Test A	135
Tracking progress	138
Test B	139
Answers and mark scheme – Test B	155
Tracking progress	158
Test C	159
Answers and mark scheme – Test C	173
Tracking progress	176

© Copyright HeadStart Primary Ltd 2016

INTRODUCTION

HeadStart Primary English Reading Comprehension has been produced to make the teacher's formative assessment of reading as straightforward as possible. At the same time, its aim is to develop children's reading skills and encourage their engagement with literature in all its forms.

With this in mind, sections have been organised to follow closely the National Curriculum and the different reading skills (content domains) highlighted in the KS2 English Reading Test Framework 2016 (available to download at www.gov.uk), with an emphasis on **comprehension, making inferences, language for effect** and **themes and conventions**.

The tasks presented here increase in difficulty as you work through a section. This allows for:

- easier access for the child still acquiring and developing basic skills
- a challenge for the child whose skills are more secure
- a further challenge and consolidation for the child who is in the process of exceeding year group expectations.

This will enable the teacher to monitor the progress a child is making in each particular skill area, thereby easing the process of formative assessment and subsequent planning. An individual child, for instance, may have a wide vocabulary but lack inferential skills. The organisation of tasks will make this apparent so that the child's learning can be moved forward.

A range of fiction and non-fiction underpins the reading tasks as well as the range of texts in the **TESTS** section. Since the removal of national curriculum levels, schools are now free to choose their own methods of monitoring progress in reading. The tests here have been provided to help the process of formative assessment, but they could be used simply to give children experience of the test format. This is for the professional judgement of the class teacher. It is worth noting that, where a school is using the tests to monitor progress year by year, the tests provided here do, in fact, offer coverage of the different reading skills comparable to the SATs tests. This means the highest percentage of questions relate to domains 2b (retrieving information) and 2d (making and justifying inferences), followed by 2a (words in context), 2c (summarising main ideas), followed by the other domains.

For complete flexibility, the accompanying CD-ROM includes not only a copy of the book in colour for use on the interactive whiteboard, but also an answer book.

Finally, the texts have been chosen in relation to Year 5 subject areas, their age-appropriate spelling lists and with the enjoyment of reading in mind.

Words in context

Strand: Comprehension

National Curriculum reference:

- checking that the text makes sense to them

Reading Test / Content Domain links: 2a, 2b

MARKING HOMEWORK

You are the teacher. Someone has handed in their homework about a birthday party. Their spelling is good. The main problem is they've chosen the wrong words for the context. Correct them by finding the wrong words and writing the correct one above. The words that need correcting are in **bold**.

My Birthday Surprise

I must have been thinking **allowed** when I walked **thorough** the front door, because there was silence **threw** out the house. I **guest** the family was up to something. It was my birthday, after all. What I didn't know was **weather** everyone was in the living room or hiding in the kitchen.

"Oh! I wonder **were** they can all be!" I shouted very dramatically. Nobody I know likes **particle** jokes more than **are** dad.

As I **past** the kitchen door, I **fought** I heard my baby brother making a gurgling sound. But when I peered round the door, all I could see was the cat licking the dripping tap and a note that said: 'All gone out for a **piazza**. See you later.'

ALADDIN IS INGENIOUS

There are many versions of Aladdin – a Middle Eastern folktale which is part of The Book of One Thousand and One Nights. Here is one. Use the list of words to fill in the gaps and make sense of the story.

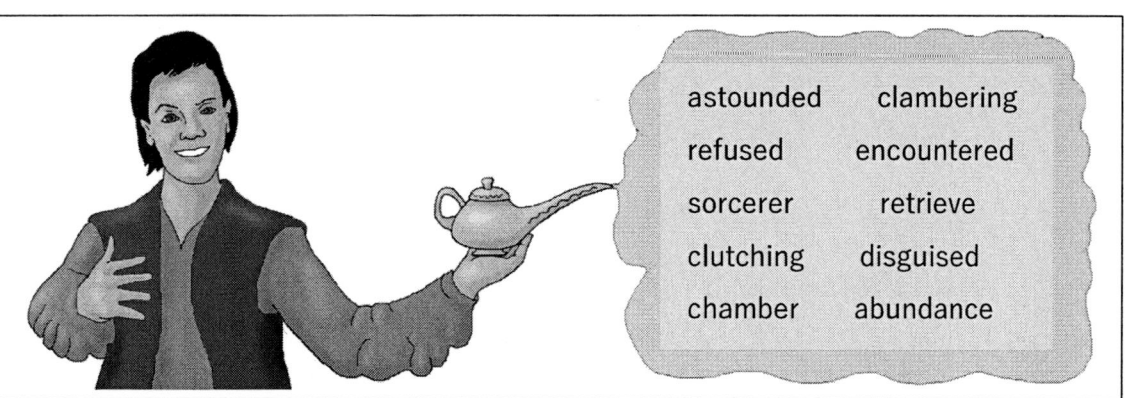

astounded   clambering
refused   encountered
sorcerer   retrieve
clutching   disguised
chamber   abundance

Once, in a distant land, there lived a poor widow who had an only son called Aladdin. Picking figs to earn some money, he _____ a _____ who was _____ as a weary traveller.

"I will give you this silver piece if you help me roll the boulder aside, climb down into that cave and _____ something for me." When he was offered a magic ring for protection, the boy agreed.

_____ down into the darkness, Aladdin found himself in a large _____ filled with an _____ of glittering jewels. Aladdin was about to fill his pockets with the wonderful, sparkling gems when a voice from above called: "Leave those and bring me the old oil lamp!"

When Aladdin reached the mouth of the cave, the old man wouldn't let him out until he handed over the lamp. When Aladdin _____, the old man pushed back the boulder. Aladdin was trapped. But when he rubbed the ring accidentally, a genie appeared. Aladdin was _____.

The genie granted Aladdin's wish to be taken home still _____ the old lamp so desired by the old, weary traveller.

NEW WORDS FOR OLD

Aladdin's story continues. After you've read it, find synonyms (words that mean the same as or are similar to) those in the table below.

When Aladdin appeared from nowhere and informed his mother of what had occurred, she was dumbfounded. Then, when she decided to clean the grimy oil lamp, they were both astonished when an even bigger and mightier genie materialised before their eyes.

Immediately, Aladdin wished for great wealth and a palace for he and his mother to live in. Soon, known all around for his generosity, he spoke to the Sultan and requested the hand of his daughter, Halima, in marriage.

The old traveller, however, came to hear about Aladdin's wealth and came to the palace dressed as a trader. On a day that Aladdin was away, the trader wandered through town calling: "New lamps for old!" Imagining her husband would be overjoyed with her action, she exchanged the magic lamp for a new one. The old man laughed pitilessly, rubbed the lamp and commanded the genie to take him, Halima and the palace to a distant land.

But Aladdin still possessed the magic ring. He asked its genie to take him to wherever Halima was kept captive. Together, they gave the old man a sleeping potion, found the lamp and returned home – palace, riches and all.

word	synonym	word	synonym
informed		wealth	
dumbfounded		imagining	
grimy		overjoyed	
materialised		exchanged	
astonished		pitilessly	
mightier		commanded	
generosity		possessed	
requested		captive	

WHO'S GOT IT RIGHT?

Here are two children talking about some television programmes they've been watching. They don't always use the correct words. Underline any wrong words that have been used and put a **tick** or a **cross** in the boxes under their speech bubbles.

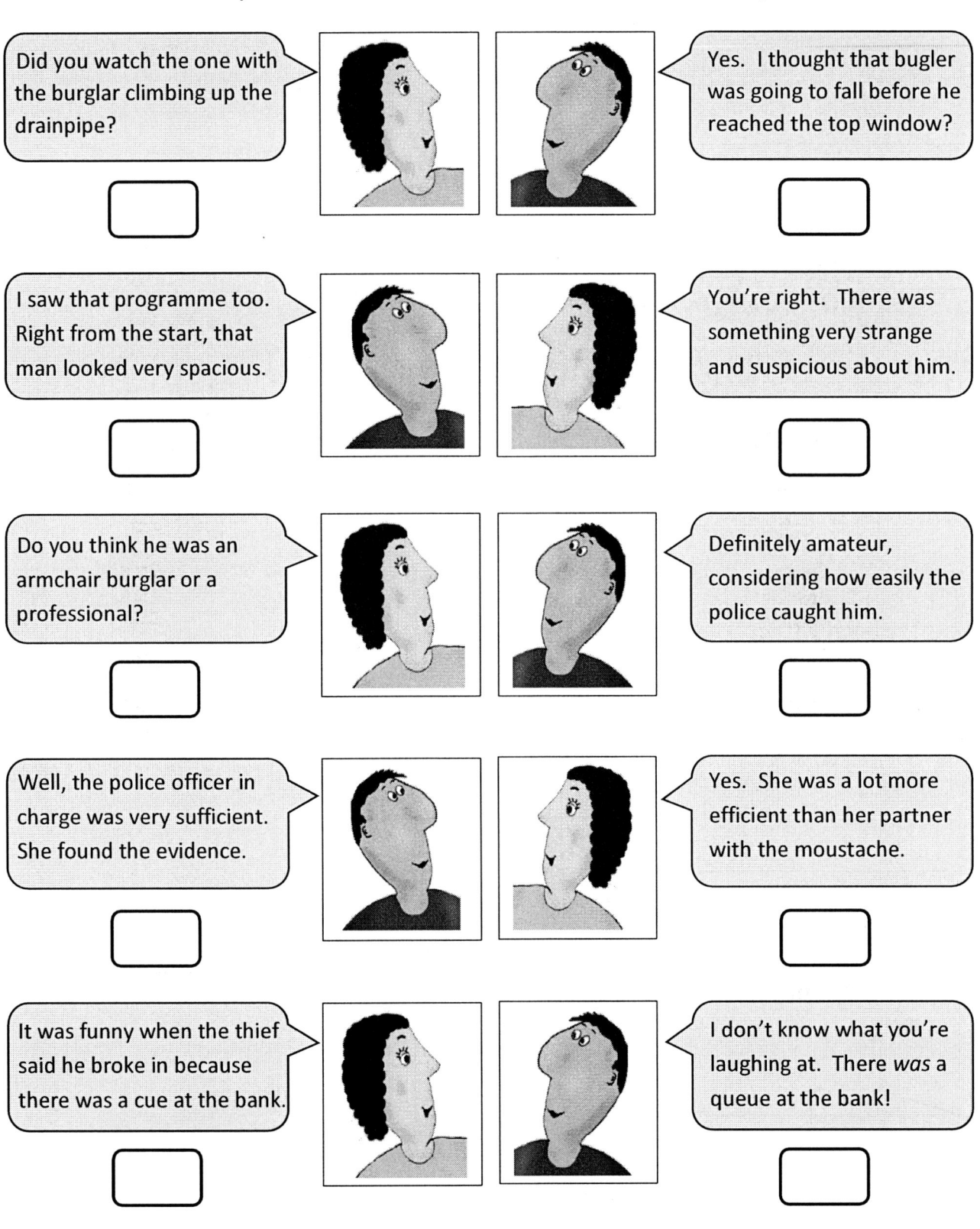

OUR HOBBIES

Jamila and Sanjeev, like different things. Here they are talking about their hobbies.

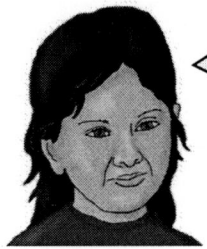

Hi. My name is Jamila. I'm very interested in anything to do with geography. All sorts of information easily stays in my memory. The names of capital cities, mountain ranges – I love all that stuff. I'd be very reluctant to stop my studies. In fact, when I'm older I hope to find a solution to some of the world's environmental problems.

1. Which word or phrase tells you how much Jamila likes her chosen hobby? _____

2. Which word tells you she likes to study different countries? _____

3. Which word tells you she has no difficulty in remembering facts about different countries? _____

4. Which word suggests she would be unwilling to give up her hobby? _____

5. Which word tells you she would like to sort out problems in the world? _____

My name is Sanjeev and my friends think I'm a bit eccentric. That's because I get up at dawn with my binoculars to do some bird-watching. It's so peaceful then. No traffic; just birdsong. Getting up at four-thirty may sound mad, but try it once in the summer holidays and you'll realise the experience is irresistible.

1. Which word tells you Sanjeev's friends think he's unusual? _____

2. What does he use to get a better view of the birds? _____

3. Which word tells you it's quiet at that time in the morning? _____

4. Which word means he can't give it up? _____

WORD SWAPPING

Read these sentences and think of a word or phrase that means the same, or is similar, to the one in **bold**. One has already been done for you.

1. I ran as fast as I could from the **venomous** snake. _____

2. I was very **thankful** when my lost cat was returned. _____

3. The food I had at the new restaurant was **delicious**. _____tasty_____

4. The headteacher told off the boy for being **impolite**. _____

5. The reckless driver **disregarded** the No Entry sign. _____

6. Even with a map, I was **uncertain** which way to go. _____

7. Who replaced Henry VIII as **monarch** when he died? _____

8. Is it as hard to **descend** a mountain as it is going up? _____

9. I had the **misfortune** of having my car keys stolen. _____

10. The twins were **quarrelling** over who owned the ball. _____

11. The children **suspended** decorations from the ceiling. _____

12. The superhero could **transform** herself into a tiger. _____

13. The parents were asked to **donate** money to charity. _____

14. Gardeners **prune** roses to encourage growth. _____

15. I was happy to **exchange** my old pen for a new one. _____

© Copyright HeadStart Primary Ltd 2016

IN THE DOG HOUSE

Here is Matt's description of his first day working at weekends at the local dogs' home. Use the list of words to fill in the gaps in his account.

My sister said, "Matt, if you call yourself an animal-lover, and you want to earn some money, then you should get a weekend job taking the dogs out for a walk down at Mallory's Motel for Malevolent Mutts."

All week, my _____ bothered me. She was right. Not only did I need money to buy a new _____ for my drum kit, I spent most weekends totally _____ .

When I phoned up, I didn't need to _____ Mr Mallory to take me on. He was delighted. He did say that some of the dogs, especially one called Killer did have a bit of a reputation for being rather _____ , but not to worry.

My knees were shaking as I walked down there... right next door to the _____ - not a good sign. When I saw Killer, I just wondered what he must _____ . He was huge. A pile of _____ and teeth. Then he took a step towards me and licked my face. Phew! Such an _____ dog.

WORD CHOICES

Read these sentences and **draw a circle** round the word that makes sense in the context, i.e. that fits in with the meaning of the sentence. A dictionary might be useful if you're stuck.

1. When you've been working hard on your homework, do you feel **exhausted** or **exorbitant**?

2. If someone pulled up the daffodils in your front garden, would it be a **suspicious** or a **malicious** thing to do?

3. If a racing driver was going at great speed, would spectators be impressed by his **velocity** or his **veracity**?

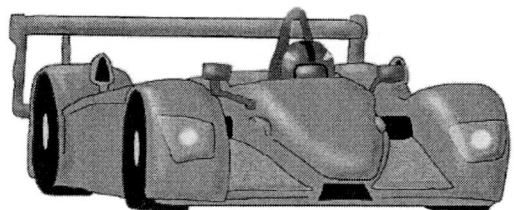

4. When a doctor wears gloves to do an examination, is it because he thinks the germs might be **infectious** or **fictitious**?

5. If a child said she liked chocolate more than toffee, would she be expressing her **reference** or her **preference**?

6. When a group of children are able to work together in class without falling out, are they showing how well they can **co-operate** or how well they can **correspond**?

7. Sometimes, a TV ad can make you rush out and buy some new product. Is the ad being **pervasive** or **persuasive**?

8. When you had that terrible meal in the restaurant, would you say it was **indelible** or **inedible**?

9. If you were the new kid at school and everybody in your class wanted to be your friend, would you feel **accepted, excepted** or **expected**?

Explaining words in context

Strand: Comprehension

National Curriculum reference:

- [checking that the text makes sense to them], discussing their understanding, and explaining the meaning of words in context

Reading Test / Content Domain links: 2a, 2b, 2f

MISSING WORDS

Complete these sentences, using the context to help you choose the correct word from the list. In each sentence, particular key words or phrase will give you a clue. **Underline** the words or phrases that help you make the right choice.

1. In a medical _____ , I'd call an ambulance.

2. I need to buy some _____ batteries for my torch that's stopped working.

3. My socks must be very _____ , because they soak up lots of water.

4. Because I love science and I'm very _____ I'll pass the exam.

5. A _____ in the cost of cinema tickets resulted in more people going.

6. An _____ of the rugby player's injured leg showed that no bones were broken.

7. There seems to be _____ over who the pencil case belongs to, as Jan and Rula both have the same design.

8. Finally, I've gathered together all the _____ I'll need for my camping holiday.

9. Trout are very cunning, so it takes a lot of _____ to sit on the riverbank all day, hoping to catch one.

10. My dog was very _____ to try the cheaper dogfood I bought.

| examination | confident | reluctant | confusion | replacement |
| emergency | absorbent | reduction | patience | equipment |

© Copyright HeadStart Primary Ltd 2016

IF I MET A SNAKE

This poem plays with words. Read the first two lines to see how it works. Then, using the word list provided, fill in the blanks. (There are extra words you might not need.) When you've finished, explain why you chose those particular words.

If I Met a Snake

If I met a slithering snake, I would recoil in horror.
If the potatoes were overdone, I'd surely boil with rage.
If the lemonade was flat, I'd quietly _____ with anger.
If I met my favourite film star, I'd hope to _____ my age.

If I had a cuddly piglet, I'd easily _____ with delight.
If I lost my old dog, Henry, I'd _____ up the wrong tree.
If a tiger told a silly joke, I might _____ with laughter.
If I felt the Earth rumble, I would _____ nervously.

If I missed the ball at cricket, I'd _____ the nearest bus.
If our rugby team was losing, I'd _____ to hide my fears.
If I dropped My auntie's china, I'd _____ into a sweat.
If I saw my bungalow fall down, I'd _____ into tears.

If I were a terrible goalkeeper, I'd _____ my energy.
If I couldn't join the orchestra, I'd surely _____ the fool.
If your nose dribbles in my direction, I would _____ a mile.
If an Olympic athlete visited, I'd _____ for joy at school.

quake
roar
jump
shout
fizz
break
squeal
slide
catch
bark
act
save
play
dive
try
run
collapse

This is why I chose those words:

_____
_____
_____

© Copyright HeadStart Primary Ltd 2016

SUN, EARTH AND MOON

Read this information about the Sun, Earth and Moon. Then look at the meanings given in the table below. Find the relevant words in the text.

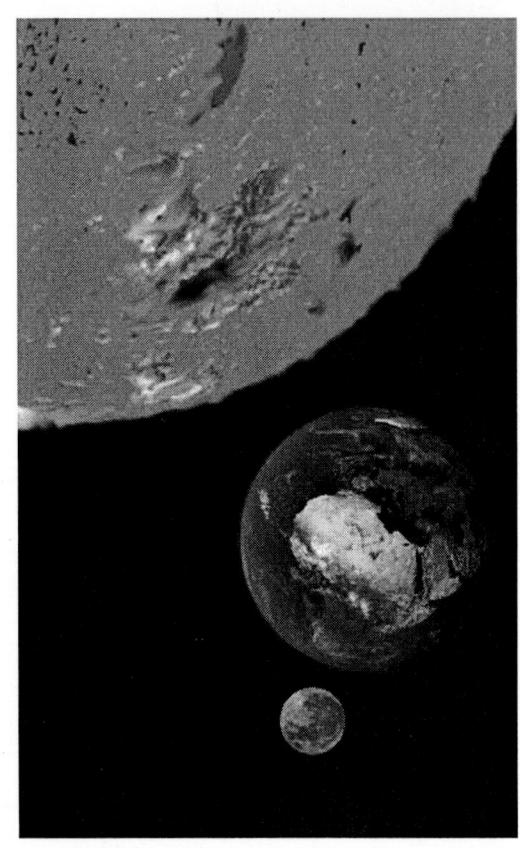

At the centre of our solar system is our nearest star, the Sun. It is composed mainly of two gases: hydrogen and helium. Approximately one million Earths would fit inside the Sun. It takes 365 days for our planet to orbit the Sun.

The Earth has its own satellite: the Moon. Its orbit of the Earth takes 27.3 days. It is not a source of light. Instead it reflects light from the Sun. Recent discoveries have shown that the Moon has some atmosphere, but no air we could breathe. Scientists believe that its craters were caused by the impact of meteorites hitting its surface.

The Earth is one of eight planets orbiting the Sun. (Pluto was once classified as a planet until recently.) One significant feature of the Earth is that about 71% of its surface is covered with water. Water is an essential requirement for life.

Now find words that have the meanings shown in the table:

meaning	word
be made of	
almost exactly	
take a path round an object in space	
an object in space that revolves round a planet	
the gases surrounding a planet or moon	
the striking of one thing against another	
identified as part of a group	
important	
absolutely necessary	

RHINOS

Read this information about rhinoceroses, then complete the table below, explaining what the words mean. If you're unsure, read the relevant sentence again.

You can identify members of the rhinoceros family by their large dimensions, their diet of plants, and thick, protective hide. Although the skin may resemble armour-plating, it is very sensitive to sunburn and insect bites. This is the reason they wallow around in mud, which acts as extra protection.

The name *rhinoceros* comes from two Greek words: *rhino* (nose) and *ceros* (horn). Rhino horns are not bone and continue to grow throughout their lifetime. Horns are composed of a protein called keratin, which is the same substance that hair and fingernails are made from.

Rhinos have well-developed senses of hearing and smell, but poor eyesight. If you were to stand motionless, even as close as thirty metres away, you might not be detected (unless you smelled awful). If you were to make a sound, however, you would immediately be in danger. In that situation, finding a tree to climb is a better strategy than trying to outrun them. They can run at between 30 and 40 mph!

word	meaning
identify	
dimensions	
protective	
hide	
diet	
resemble	
wallow	
composed	
substance	
continue	
detected	
strategy	

Retrieving and recording information

Strand: Comprehension

National Curriculum reference:

- retrieving and recording information / identifying key details from fiction and non-fiction

Reading Test / Content Domain links: 2a, 2b

ISLAND RETREATS

Look at the holiday centres on these islands and, if they can offer what is shown in the table below, give it a **tick**.

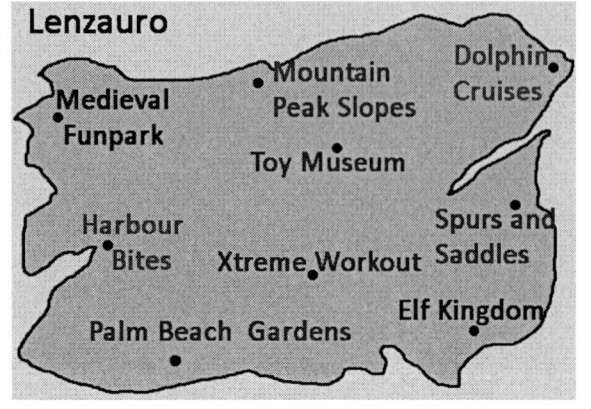
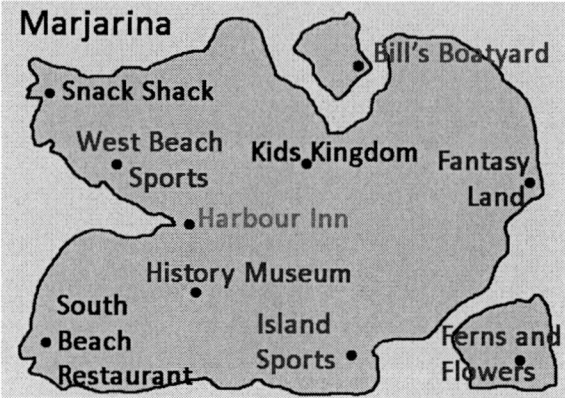
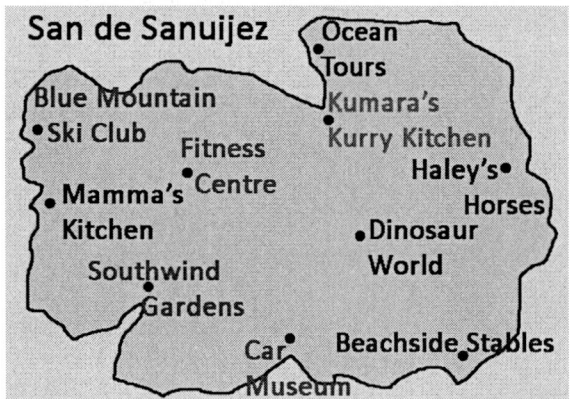
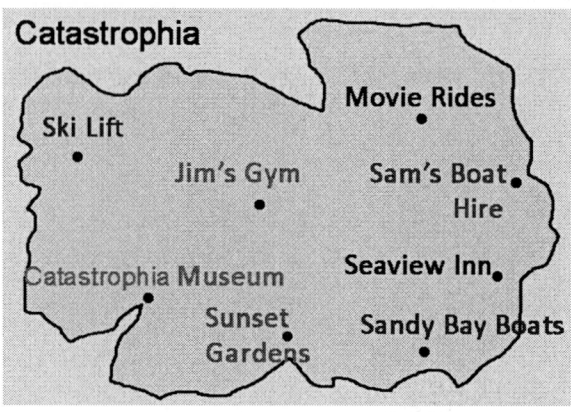

activity	Lenzauro	Marjarina	San de Sanuijez	Catastrophia
museums				
tropical gardens				
theme parks				
boat trips				
sports centres				
restaurants				
ski slopes				
riding clubs				

PLANETARY FACTS

Here are some facts about the planets nearest to the Earth.

Named after the Roman messenger to the gods, Mercury is the smallest planet and the closest to the Sun. Thirteen times a century, it passes in front of the Sun. This is called a *transit*. The next time is 9th May 2016.
Moons: none.
Orbit period: 1 Mercury year = 88 Earth days.
Surface temperature: 427° C facing the Sun and -173° C away from the Sun, due to the planet having very little atmosphere.

Named after the Roman goddess of love, Venus is the second planet from the Sun, can be seen as a bright object in the sky, and is similar in size to the Earth.
Moons: none.
Orbit period: 1 Venus year = 224.7 Earth days.
Surface temperature: 462° C. Its covering of cloud layers creates a greenhouse effect, trapping the heat. It is thought that Venus once had oceans but as the planet's temperature increased, they evaporated.

Named after the Roman god of war, Mars is the fourth planet from the Sun. Reddish in appearance, it is called the Red Planet. Recently, signs of water have been found.
Moons: two – Phobos and Deimos.
Orbit period: 1 Mars year = 687 Earth days.
Surface temperature: -5° C to -87° C. Mars has been volcanic in the past. It has the biggest dust storms in the solar system, sometimes lasting for months and covering the entire surface of the planet.

Named after the king of the Roman gods, Jupiter is the fifth planet from the Sun, and two-and-a-half times more massive than all the other planets in the solar system combined. Its Great Red Spot is a storm that has raged for at least 350 years.
Moons: 67, including Io, Calisto, Europa and Ganymede. (It is thought that Europa has water under a frozen surface.)
Orbit period: 1 Jupiter year = 11.86 Earth years.
Surface temperature: -108° C.

© Copyright HeadStart Primary Ltd 2016

1. Which of these four planets is the smallest?

   _____

2. Which planet is similar to the Earth in size?

   _____

3. Which planets have moons?

   _____

4. Which planet has the hottest surface temperature?

   _____

5. Keeping in mind that Earth takes 365 days to orbit the Sun, which of these planets take longer to orbit the Sun than the Earth?

   _____

6. **Two** of the planets experience different kinds of storms. Which planets?

   _____

7. Name the **two** places where astronomers have discovered evidence of water.

   _____

8. How often does Mercury pass between us and the Sun?

   _____

9. Draw lines to match up the planets with what they meant in Roman times.

Jupiter	Goddess of love
Mars	Messenger of the gods
Venus	King of the gods
Mercury	God of war

BOUDICCA – WHO'S WHO?

Here is some information about events and the people in the life of Boudicca. Underlining the key characters will help you answer the questions that follow.

Boudicca

Before the Romans arrived in Britain, different parts of the country were controlled by different Celtic tribes: the Iceni, for instance, in what is now known as East Anglia, and the Trinovantes in an area north of the Thames estuary. Often they traded; sometimes they fought against each other.

The ruler of the Iceni was Prasutagus, the husband of Boudicca. When the Romans conquered the south of England in AD 43, Prasutagus was permitted to carry on ruling. When he died, however, the Romans took direct control, plundering Iceni lands and property. The tribes began to resent the Romans.

At first, the Celtic tribes had great success, defeating the Roman Ninth Legion and destroying the Roman capital of Camulodunum (Colchester). This was followed by victories at Londinium (London) and Verulamium (St Albans). The Roman Governor of Britain at the time, Gaius Suetonius Paulinus, was forced to retreat.

The Roman historian, Tacitus, has provided us with an account of a battle that took place around AD 61.

It has been said that Boudicca prayed to Andrasta, the Celtic goddess of war, before facing the reinforcements that Governor Paulinus put together. Yet, even heavily outnumbering the Romans, the Iceni and the other tribes were no match for the Romans' discipline, weaponry and cavalry. It was a massacre. What happened to Boudicca, no one can be certain. Was she killed in battle or taken prisoner? Some say she took her own life.

Her determination and bravery live on. In 1902, a bronze statue of the Warrior Queen riding in her chariot, designed by Thomas Thornycroft, was erected near the Houses of Parliament in London.

Now complete the table below, saying who each person was.

name	who or what were they?
Iceni	
Prasutagus	
Trinovantes	
Camulodunum	
Londinium	
Verulamium	
Gaius Suetonius Paulinus	
Tacitus	
Andrasta	
Thomas Thornycroft	
Warrior Queen	

DRUMS AND DRUMMING

Here is some information about drums and how widely they have been used.

HISTORY

Drums are among the oldest of musical instruments, dating approximately from 5000 BC in the Middle East, China and India. Drums have been used not just for music, but also in religious ceremonies and to communicate over long distances. A good example of this is the African **talking drum**, which imitates the sounds of the human voice.

MILITARY USES

The Chinese used drums to motivate their soldiers, set a marching pace and to transmit orders. Aztecs in battle were known to communicate to their warriors by means of drumming. The same is true of British forces in the past, when the sound of a drum could be heard over the noise of battle.

DRUM DESIGN

The design of drums hasn't changed much over the years, consisting of at least one drum skin, or membrane, stretched over a cylinder made of wood, metal or plant gourd. The sound – percussion – is created by striking with the hand or by using a stick or sticks. A set of different drums together plus cymbals form the modern drum kit.

ANIMAL DRUMMERS

Some apes send out a message of their dominance by beating their chest or clapping. Rodents, such as Kangaroo Rats, perform a similar action – sometimes when danger is near – by drumming their paws on the ground.

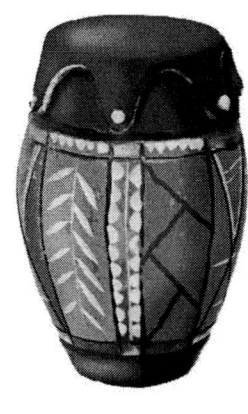
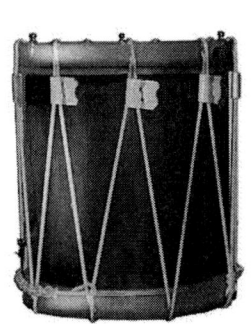

1. Where has evidence of the earliest drums been found?
   _____

2. What is distinctive about the talking drum?
   _____

3. Describe **three** ways in which drums have been used in battle.
   _____

   _____

   _____

4. What is a **membrane**?
   _____

5. What materials might be used in the making of a drum?
   _____

6. What is the word that means the striking of a drum to produce a sound?
   _____

7. How does the modern drum kit differ from single drums?
   _____

   _____

8. Which animals use drumming to communicate?
   _____

9. Explain why animals make drumming sounds.
   _____

   _____

THE HORSE TRAINER

Here are some tips on how to train a horse. Follow the instructions and answer the questions that follow.

SAFETY GUIDELINES

Always remember that you are dealing with a big, powerful animal. It is extremely important that you stand where your horse can see you. The first thing that any experienced horse trainers will tell you is: never walk behind your horse. Walk around in front of it. If it's absolutely necessary to be close to it but out of its sight, remember to keep talking so that it knows where you are.

Another method is to run your hand down its side to signal where you're going. If you are working with its head, stand on its left (known as the *near*side), in line with its ear and at an angle. It can see you best there. Should your horse be suddenly startled, you are in a good position to get out of its way.

Above all, never kneel or sit on the floor near it. That will most likely lead to an accident, and the fault will be yours, not your horse's.

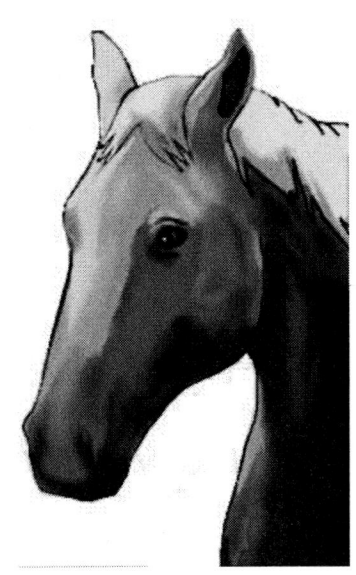

PATIENCE AND PERSISTENCE

If you wish to teach your horse a new skill or change its behaviour, take it slowly one step at a time. Never raise your voice or get angry, not if you want a calm, confident animal. Respond to your horse when it does what you want by immediately rewarding it so that the behaviour will be repeated next time you ask. This is called *reinforcement*.

There are two kinds of reinforcement: *positive* and *negative*. (These don't necessarily mean *good* and *bad*.) Positive reinforcers include treats, speaking softly or stroking. It should be given the instant your horse does what you want. Negative reinforcers are things like a gentle push with the fingers, a light tap of the whip, or rein or leg pressure. They are never abrupt and never frightening or painful for the horse. Negative reinforcement should continue until the horse gives the right response. Remember: be patient but persistent.

1. What important advice are you likely to receive from an experienced horse trainer?

2. Describe two ways of letting your horse know where you are, if it can't see you.

3. When dealing with a horse, what is meant by the *nearside*?

4. Why is it important to remain standing while looking after a horse?

5. What would be the result if you were to get angry with your horse and shout?

6. How does rewarding your horse for the behaviour you want lead to success in training?

7. Describe three examples of positive reinforcement.

8. Describe three examples of negative reinforcement.

9. Positive and negative reinforcements are used differently. Explain how they should be used.

THE TOWER OF LONDON

After a school trip to the Tower of London, these children gave a short presentation in assembly. They each chose a topic that interested them.

After William the Conqueror defeated King Harold at the Battle of Hastings, he needed castles and towers to protect himself and keep control of England. The Tower of London was one of those buildings.

The first person to be imprisoned in the White Tower was Ranulf Flambard. He was the Bishop of Durham and the chief tax collector. He had made himself very rich and King Henry I accused him of extortion (forcing people to hand over more money to him than they needed to).  One night, while a feast was going, he had friends smuggle in a rope inside a gallon of wine. Inviting his guards to join him, he soon got them drunk. Then he used the rope to let himself down from a window. Outside, his friends were waiting with horses; and so he also became the first person to escape from the tower.

Many years ago, according to a legend, an enormous, ghostly bear appeared beside the Martin Tower. It frightened a guard to death! Literally! He dropped down dead on the spot. Now you might think: "What would a bear be doing there?" Well, in 1251, King Henry III received a present from the King of Norway. It was a polar bear and a long chain was attached to a collar, so that it could hunt for fish in the River Thames. Maybe the guard was scared by the real bear: it was white and he wouldn't have seen one before. The ghost hasn't been seen since.

The Tower of London had been standing for 400 years when Henry VIII was born. He used it for all sorts of things, such as a fortress and a prison. He also used it as a storehouse for his own precious possessions. In fact, he and Anne Boleyn lived there for a while. He had coins minted there and even kept a menagerie of wild animals there.

© Copyright HeadStart Primary Ltd 2016

1. Why did William the Conqueror order the construction of the Tower of London?
   _____

2. Ranulf Flambard held two important positions. What were they?
   _____
   _____

3. What does **extortion** mean?
   _____
   _____

4. Sanjeev suggests that Ranulf Flambard has two 'firsts' – two records. What are they?
   _____
   _____

5. What phrase suggests that Hannah doubts the story of the ghostly bear?
   _____

6. What is Hannah's explanation for the guard being scared to death?
   _____
   _____

7. Seth says the Tower of London has had many uses. **Tick** the ones he mentions.

storage of vegetables	☐	prison	☐
minting coins	☐	games room	☐
fortress	☐	menagerie	☐
storehouse for possessions	☐	living accommodation	☐

WALTER RALEIGH

Walter Raleigh is known for introducing the potato and tobacco to Britain. It seems he would have preferred to have found gold in South America. Read these details of his life, then answer the questions that follow.

Walter Raleigh

Queen Elizabeth I

King James I

Walter Raleigh and El Dorado

Born in Devon around 1552, Walter Raleigh had a lifelong interest in America, or the New World as it was known. He was well-educated and a favourite of Queen Elizabeth I, especially after he quelled an uprising in Ireland in 1580. As a result, he was knighted and promoted to Captain of the Queen's Guard.

He had already sailed to America to establish a colony, but failed; and tried again a few years later without success.

He is credited with bringing back potatoes and tobacco to Europe, although the Spanish had already introduced them here. In fact, the Spanish, at the time, in conflict with England had a strong grip on parts of South America.

When the first Spanish explorers reached the continent, they heard many legends about tribes in the high Andes and their use of gold in their ceremonies. Stories varied, but it was claimed that gold played a part in the rituals of leadership. It was said that a new leader was covered in gold dust. Then gold and other precious jewels were thrown into Lake Guativita to please the underwater goddess. The Spanish called this chief *El Dorado* – the Golden One. Soon, it became the name of a mysterious city of gold.

Meanwhile, Raleigh fell into disfavour with Elizabeth when he married one of her maids of honour without asking the Queen's permission. In a rage, Elizabeth imprisoned them both in the Tower of London – not in a dungeon, but in some comfortable rooms.

When he was released, Raleigh hoped to regain the Queen's favour by setting off to find the fabled city of El Dorado. Raleigh sailed to the River Orinoco and beyond, but failed to find any gold.

James I, who succeeded Elizabeth I, did not trust Raleigh, who was accused (probably falsely) of plotting against the King. Once more, he was thrown into prison in the Tower. This time, he spent 12 years locked up. In 1616, James, in need of money, agreed to let Raleigh, now an old man, try again to find El Dorado. The one condition was that there should be no conflict with the Spanish.

The expedition was a total disaster. Raleigh's son was killed in a battle with the Spanish. Raleigh, having defied the King, returned in October 1618 without any gold, to face a death sentence. As his executioner hesitated, Raleigh said: "This is sharp medicine; but it is a sure cure for all diseases…"

1. Why does the writer say that Walter Raleigh was born **around** 1552?

2. How did Queen Elizabeth I reward Raleigh for dealing with the uprising in Ireland?

3. Raleigh was rewarded for his successes. He also experienced some major failures. What were they?

4. What other word in the text is similar in meaning to **ceremonies**?

5. The stories and legends of tribal chiefs in the Andes might not have been true. What are the **two** phrases that are used to suggest they might not be true?

6. Describe the tribal leadership ceremony.

   _____

   _____

7. Today, El Dorado is thought of as a lost city of gold. What did it mean originally?

   _____

8. Why did Elizabeth I imprison Raleigh in the Tower of London?

   _____

9. Why did James I imprison Raleigh in the Tower of London?

   _____

10. What words suggest that Raleigh might have been innocent?

    _____

11. The text describes **three** ways in which 'The expedition was a total disaster'. What were they?

    _____

    _____

    _____

12. What was the 'sharp medicine' that Raleigh referred to on the day of his execution?

    _____

13. Why do you think it was a 'sure cure for all diseases'?

    _____

    _____

Fact and opinion

Strand: Comprehension

National Curriculum reference:

- retrieving and recording information from non-fiction
- distinguishing between statements of fact and opinion

Reading Test / Content Domain links: 2a, 2b, 2g

WANTED

Here are wanted posters of some odd characters. Their descriptions contain a few **opinions** as well as **facts**. Can you separate the opinions from the facts?

WANTED: TROLL

Height: 4 feet 9¼ inches.
Appearance: quite ugly – should visit a dentist soon.
Crime: being a menace to people crossing his bridge, especially Billy Goats.
Note: probably needs a few friends. Any volunteers?

WANTED: STEP-MOTHER (WICKED)

Height: 5 feet 6 inches (in high heels).
Appearance: I'd say not as gorgeous as she thinks she is. (Ask her mirror!)
Crime: not nice to her step-daughter.
Note: should try knitting.

WANTED: GIANT

Height: 19 feet 8 inches (in his socks).
Appearance: he looks far too big for his boots.
Crime: frightening Jack and other Englishmen.
Note: can be reached by beanstalk.

WANTED: GOLDILOCKS

Height: 6 feet (when standing on a chair).
Appearance: lots of golden hair and a bit prim.
Crime: destroying the furniture of a law-abiding family of bears.
Note: she must hate muesli.

WANTED: BIG BAD WOLF

Height: 3 feet 11 inches.
Appearance: you could say he looks charming but I'm not keen on those teeth.
Crime: the list is too long!
Note: keeps turning up in fairytales despite best efforts of the woodcutter.

WANTED: WITCH

Height: 5 feet 1½ inches (including pointy hat).
Appearance: bad teeth, cackling laugh, occasional wart on the nose.
Crime: horrid to kids, puts people to sleep, etc.
Note: good at spelling.

Now read the statements in this table and put a **tick** under **fact** or **opinion**.

TROLL	fact	opinion
should visit a dentist soon		
being a menace to people crossing his bridge		
probably needs a few friends		

WICKED STEPMOTHER	fact	opinion
5 feet 6 inches (in high heels)		
I'd say not as gorgeous as she thinks she is		
not nice to her step-daughter		

GIANT	fact	opinion
he looks far too big for his boots		
frightening Jack and other Englishmen		
can be reached by beanstalk		

GOLDILOCKS	fact	opinion
lots of golden hair		
destroying the furniture of a law-abiding family of bears		
she must hate muesli		

BIG BAD WOLF	fact	opinion
you could say he looks charming		
I'm not keen on those teeth		
he keeps turning up in fairytales		

WITCH	fact	opinion
bad teeth, cackling laugh, occasional wart on the nose		
horrid to kids		
puts people to sleep, etc.		

VULTURES

Vultures are not the cuddliest of creatures. There are some facts and opinions in the following description of them. Look at the list of statements below and write **fact** or **opinion** after them

- Vultures are large, carnivorous birds. _____

- They are found all around the world except Australia and Antarctica. _____

- We are very fortunate not to have any in the wild in Britain. _____

- There are around 30 different species of vulture. _____

- They scavenge for food rather than killing animals themselves. _____

- It must be scary for dying animals seeing vultures circling overhead. _____

- Their eyesight must be amazing if they're able to see their prey three or four miles away. _____

- New World Vultures (those in N. and S. America) are smaller than those in Africa, Asia and Europe. _____

- Having no feathers on their heads makes them look very ugly. _____

- They do an excellent job clearing up dead animals. _____

GAME REVIEWS

People have different views about computer games. Read this game review and decide which statements in the table below are **facts** and which are personal **opinions**. **Tick** the correct boxes.

> I have to say, after playing this game for an hour, blowing up the Mercury Men everywhere, I began to feel sorry for the dragon. The dragon, or Draco, as he is known, is surrounded by these Mercury characters who keep changing shape: one minute, a tree, the next minute, a cat. Whatever their disguise, they're a bit weird. They are Draco's guards, but, by the time, you reach Draco's castle, you wonder if they are actually keeping him imprisoned. Reaching the castle is made even trickier by the Gargoyles. I'll leave you to find out for yourself what powers they have. Dracoworld is action-packed, the movement is sharp and the graphics clear. As far as I'm concerned, it's challenging and fun. I recommend it.

statement	fact	opinion
playing this game for an hour		
I began to feel sorry for the dragon		
The dragon is surrounded by these Mercury characters		
one minute, a tree, the next minute a cat		
Whatever their disguise, they're a bit weird		
They are Draco's guards		
you wonder if they're actually keeping him imprisoned		
Dracoworld is action-packed		
it's challenging and fun		

CHINESE NEW YEAR

Here is Lian describing what happens in her house at New Year.

> The evening before the Chinese New Year is great. We all get together for a big, family reunion dinner. Traditionally, we clean the house from top to bottom. I can't say my brother, Chen, does his share. Anyway, it symbolises sweeping away bad luck and preparing to welcome good luck. We decorate the doors and windows with red paper cut-outs. My cutting is not very neat, but I'm getting better. The story goes that there was a mythical creature, called Nian – a bit scary, if you ask me – that appeared on the first day of New Year to eat our farm animals, corn and, especially, children. See what I mean? One of the gods, however, told a villager that Nian hated the colour red and was frightened of firecrackers. So that's what he did and Nian never returned. That's why we have red lanterns and decorations, and light firecrackers at Chinese New Year. Maybe that's why we have to be nice to brothers as well.

Write an **f** for **fact** or an **o** for **opinion** after each statement.

The evening before Chinese New Year is great ☐

We clean the house from top to bottom ☐

I can't say my brother, Chen, does his share ☐

It symbolises sweeping away bad luck ☐

My cutting is not very neat ☐

That's why we have red lanterns ☐

Maybe that's why we have to be nice to brothers ☐

The main idea

Strand: Comprehension

National Curriculum reference:

- identifying main ideas drawn from more than one paragraph

Reading Test / Content Domain links: 2a, 2b, 2c, 2f

THE EIFFEL TOWER

Here is an information leaflet about the Eiffel Tower. What is it mainly about?

The Eiffel Tower

Erected in 1889 and named after its engineer, Alexandre Gustave Eiffel, the Eiffel Tower is the most visited monument in the world. The tower welcomed its 250 millionth visitor in 2010.

The greatest number of visitors (taking on the 300 steps to the first level and another 300 to the second level, before taking a lift to the top of the tallest structure in Paris) are from France. This accounts for around 10% and is closely followed by holidaymakers from Spain, Italy, the USA and Britain.

When it opened, famous visitors included the Prince of Wales, Thomas Edison – known for inventing the world's first practical electric lightbulb, and Buffalo Bill.

What is the leaflet mainly about? Tick the correct one.

It was named after its engineer ☐

Visitors to the Eiffel Tower ☐

The tallest structure in Paris ☐

Write **two** sentences from the leaflet that helped you to make your choice:

_____

_____

_____

THE STATUE OF LIBERTY

Here is an information leaflet about the Statue of Liberty. What is it mainly about?

The Statue of Liberty

Built on Liberty Island in New York Harbour by Gustave Eiffel in 1886, the Statue of Liberty was a gift from the people of France to the USA. Some of the money for it was raised in France.

The sculpture is of a female figure representing Libertas, the Roman goddess of freedom. She wears a long robe and holds a torch as if lighting the way and a tablet of stone symbolising the law. At her feet are broken chains, also suggesting freedom.

Often referred to as *Liberty Enlightening the World*, the statue must have been a welcoming sight to migrants fleeing to the safety of the USA from European tyrants.

What is the leaflet mainly about? Tick the correct one.

- The statue is in New York harbour ☐
- It was constructed in France ☐
- It represents freedom ☐

Write **two** sentences from the leaflet that helped you to make your choice:

_____
_____
_____

IDEAS ABOUT MUSIC

Read this information about making music. Then, alongside each statement, write down whether it is the **main idea** or a **detail** that supports the main idea.

> There are a few ways you can change the pitch of a guitar string. You can tighten it or make it shorter. You can also use a thinner string.

you can change the pitch of a guitar string _____

you can tighten it or make it shorter _____

you can use a thinner string _____

> You pluck a guitar string to make it vibrate. When playing a xylophone, you strike the bars. To produce a sound, you have to create a vibration.

you pluck a guitar string to make it vibrate _____

when playing a xylophone, you strike the bars _____

to produce a sound, you have to create a vibration _____

> Stringed instruments can be plucked harder. Percussion instruments can be struck harder. This is how we change the volume of a note.

stringed instruments can be plucked harder _____

percussion instruments can be struck harder _____

this is how we change the volume of a note _____

> You can make your own instruments. It is important to gather together the right materials. Tins, rubber bands, balloons and seeds are useful.

you can make your own instruments _____

gather together the right materials _____

tins, rubber bands, balloons and seeds are useful _____

SCHOOL DAYS

Here, children from different countries are describing what school is like. Alongside what each one says, **tick** the **main idea**.

Food and eating together as a family is a big thing in Spain. My grandparents like to prepare food so we can eat lunch together. So our lunch break lasts from 12 noon till 3pm. Then school finishes at 5pm.

school day fits family life ☐

grandparents prepare food ☐

school finishes at 5pm ☐

You're not forced to wear a school uniform, but most schools in Australia have them. Because it's hot, teacher says "No hat, no play!" So, if we don't bring a hat in the summer, we don't get out at breaktime.

uniform is not compulsory ☐

it's hot in Australia ☐

clothes to wear at school ☐

In Brazil, in the schoolyard, I like to play Queimada. It means 'Burnt.' If you touch the ball when the other team throws it, we say you are burnt and die. When everybody is 'dead', the game is over. It's great!

schools have 'schoolyards' ☐

a popular breaktime game ☐

the game needs two teams ☐

In India, if you have money, you can go to a good school. But some teachers in poor government schools don't always show up, or else they write a problem on the board and then leave. I want to learn.

schools for rich and poor ☐

teachers don't show up ☐

India has good schools ☐

THE EVOLUTION OF FOOTBALL

For hundreds of years, games involving kicking or running with a ball have taken place in many parts of the world. Read the following paragraphs and **tick** the phrase that sums up each **main idea**.

Royal Engineers AFC won the FA Cup in 1875

There were many early versions of ball games, but, in England, something resembling football became so popular in the early 1300s that King Edward II tried to ban it. He was worried that people weren't practising archery enough, at a time when he was at war with Scotland.

early versions of football ◯

football was very popular ◯

war with Scotland ◯

In spite of the attempts of other kings to ban the game, more and more people played. The trouble was, lacking in any rules, football could be very violent – some of it deliberate. Sometimes, as many as 1000 people played at a time. In the chaos, there were many injuries.

more people played ◯

it lacked rules ◯

sometimes, 1000 played

Football was very popular at public schools in the 18th century. As a result, in 1848, a meeting was held in Cambridge to agree on a set of rules. These included such things as throw-ins and goal kicks. These rules were added to in later years and set the scene for the creation of new football clubs and regional matches.

a set of rules ◯

throw-ins and goal kicks ◯

new football clubs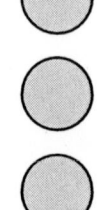

© Copyright HeadStart Primary Ltd 2016

Although football was often thought of as a male sport, since the end of the 19th century, it has been played by women as well. During the First World War, when women took on a lot of industrial jobs, many female works teams were formed. A women's team from Preston was one of the first to play in an international match against Paris in 1920.

women played as well ○

women in industrial jobs ○

Preston beat Paris ○

One football match is fast becoming legendary. It was played at Christmas in 1914. Some British soldiers in the trenches of the First World War heard some of the German army singing carols. Then both sides walked out into No Man's Land. Some played a game of football; others exchanged gifts and took photos.

a legendary match ○

Germans sang carols ○

meeting in No Man's Land ○

some played football ○

A special tournament took place in 1930 in Uruguay, who were the Olympic champions. It was here that 13 teams – 7 from South America, 4 from Europe and 2 from North America – took part in the first World Cup. Uruguay were the winners, beating Argentina 4-2 in the final. The only European teams who attended were, Belgium, France, Romania and Yugoslavia. Because of a dispute with FIFA, the ruling body, no British teams played in the first World Cup.

Olympic champions ○

the first World Cup ○

Uruguay won ○

no British team played ○

© Copyright HeadStart Primary Ltd 2016

Summarising main ideas

Strand: Comprehension

National Curriculum reference:

- identifying main ideas drawn from more than one paragraph and summarising these

Reading Test / Content Domain links: 2a, 2b, 2c, 2f

HENRY VIII

Here is some information about King Henry VIII. He was a big man and didn't like people disagreeing with him. Read about his life and the order in which various events took place.

Personal Profile:	Henry Tudor
Dates	Born in 1491 and died in 1547.
Family	When Henry was 5 years old, he and his mother, Elizabeth of York, had to flee from rebels in London to the safety of the Tower of London. His father was Henry VII and the first monarch of the House of Tudor. He died in 1509. His older brother, Arthur, would have been crowned king, but he died in 1502.
Coronation	Crowned king in 1509.
Character	Henry was a skilful horseman and archer. He enjoyed jousting, music, dancing and having feasts at Hampton Court. Making him cross risked having your head chopped off. (See 'Wives' below.)
Important actions	In 1534, he made himself Head of the Church of England. One of his warships, the Mary Rose, sank in 1545. (It was lifted off the seabed in 1982 and can be visited in Portsmouth.)
Wives	Catherine of Aragon: married in 1509 – divorced in 1533. Anne Boleyn: married in 1533 – beheaded in 1536. Jane Seymour: married in 1536 – died in 1537. Anne of Cleves: married in 1540 – divorced in 1540. Catherine Howard: married in 1540 – beheaded in 1542. Catherine Parr: married in 1543 – outlived Henry VIII, dying about 18 months after him.

Now use Henry VIII's personal profile to number the following facts in the correct order.

☐ Catherine of Aragon is divorced

☐ The Mary Rose sinks

☐ Henry VIII is born

☐ He marries Catherine Parr

☐ Henry VII dies

☐ Anne Boleyn is beheaded

☐ Henry is crowned king

☐ Henry and his mother flee to the Tower of London

☐ Henry VIII dies

☐ Henry marries Jane Seymour

☐ The Mary Rose is lifted off the seabed

☐ Henry's brother, Arthur, dies

☐ Henry divorces Anne of Cleves

☐ Catherine Howard is beheaded

NEWS HEADLINES – ROSA PARKS

Newspaper reports focus on different aspects of events depending on what appeals to their readers. Create a headline for each of these articles about Rosa Parks, whose actions helped the struggle for racial equality in the USA.

_____

_____

It could be said that Rosa Parks, brought up and educated in a segregated society in Alabama, was destined to become part of the struggle for racial equality. Much of her childhood experience was touched by discrimination. Segregated schools (i.e. separate schools for black and white children) were the rule, with black children missing out on basic equipment, such as desks.

_____

_____

In the city of Montgomery, for some time, there has existed a bus code, by which a bus driver assigns certain seats to white passengers and to black passengers. In practice, this has taken the form of a line separating white people, at the front, and African-Americans at the back. This has meant that an African-American passenger gets on at the front to pay the driver, then gets off to board again by the back door of the bus.

_____

_____

On 1st December 1955, 42-year-old Rosa Parks boarded the Cleveland Avenue bus for home after a long day at the department store, where she was employed. When she was asked by the bus driver to give up her seat to a white person, she refused. Police were called and she was arrested; subsequently, released on bail.

_____

_____

Her supporters, including Martin Luther King Jnr called for a boycott of the Montgomery bus company. For many months, buses stood empty. In June 1956, the district court declared the practice of segregation unlawful. Almost a year after Rosa's action, the US Supreme Court upheld the decision.

© Copyright HeadStart Primary Ltd 2016

THE ENDURANCE OF SHACKLETON

Ernest Shackleton is known for his heroic journey to save the stranded members of his polar expedition. Read the information, then number the events in the correct order.

Ernest Shackleton (1874 – 1922)

Ernest Henry Shackleton was born in Ireland. At the age of sixteen, he joined the merchant navy. His main ambition was to explore the poles. An opportunity came in 1901, when Captain Scott recruited him as a member of the crew of the Discovery, which set sail for the Antarctic. The aim was to be the first team to reach the South Pole, but, in extremely difficult conditions, the team failed, Shackleton became ill and had to return home.

Another attempt came in 1908 as leader of his own expedition. His came closer to the South Pole than anyone before, and, on his return, he was knighted. Three years later, the Norwegian explorer, Amundsen, was the first man to reach the pole, closely followed by Scott, who died during the homeward journey.

Shackleton made his third trip to Antarctica in 1914 on his ship, the Endurance. Early the following year, the Endurance became trapped in ice,

forcing the crew to abandon ship and seek safety on floating ice. The ship sank ten months later. This forced the team to set off in three small lifeboats for Elephant Island – a small island in the Southern Ocean. With five crew members, Shackleton took the most seaworthy of the lifeboats and set sail for South Georgia – a journey of 1300 km. After almost capsizing, they reached land.

Their mission was not over, however. They then trekked across the mountainous island until they reached a whaling station. There, Shackleton was able to organise the rescue of his men left on Elephant Island. Not one member of the Endurance expedition died, thanks to the determination of Ernest Shackleton.

Now number these events in the correct order:

☐ The Norwegian explorer, Amundsen, is the first man to reach the South Pole.

☐ Shackleton is chosen as part of Scott's team and sets sail for Antarctica on board the Discovery.

☐ Shackleton joins the merchant navy.

☐ The Endurance gets stuck in the ice and the crew have to live on the ice floe.

☐ Scott succeeds in reaching the South Pole, but dies on the journey home.

☐ Shackleton reaches a whaling station and organises the rescue of his crew.

☐ Shackleton's third trip to the Antarctic is on board the Endurance.

☐ Shackleton becomes ill during an attempt to reach the South Pole and has to return home.

☐ Shackleton's team is forced to set off for Elephant Island in three small lifeboats.

☐ Shackleton and his team have to trek across the mountainous island of South Georgia.

☐ The Endurance sinks.

☐ They set sail for South Georgia in the most seaworthy of the lifeboats.

Details that support the main idea

Strand: Comprehension

National Curriculum reference:

- identifying main ideas drawn from more than one paragraph and summarising these

Reading Test / Content Domain links: 2a, 2b, 2c, 2f

Details that support the main idea

SCIENCE HEADLINES

Here are some news headlines describing the work of scientists. **Tick** the phrase that goes with the headline.

MARS ROVER LOOKS FOR SIGNS OF LIFE ON MARS

Scientists keep their fingers crossed ☐

Liquid water is needed to support life ☐

Mars Rover had no problem landing ☐

CREATING ELEPHANT ANCESTOR IS A MAMMOTH TASK

Mammoths can survive Arctic winters ☐

Mammoths are extinct ☐

Elephants live a long time ☐

MOUNTAIN GORILLA NUMBERS DANGEROUSLY LOW

Around 880 Mountain Gorillas remaining ☐

There are different species of gorilla ☐

A dominant male is called a silverback ☐

VULTURES TURN OUT TO BE AS TOUGH AS THEY LOOK

Vultures have no feathers on their heads ☐

They have sharp claws ☐

They are able to eat rotting flesh ☐

OUR SCIENCE LESSONS

Class 5 have been doing a number of experiments and research on different science topics. Here, the children are making some statements about the human body. Draw lines to link what they say with one of the details on the right.

Exercise makes your heart beat faster and stay healthy.

Muscles are attached to bones and shorten to make them move.

One job your skeleton does is to enable you to move.

Your heart is well protected by your ribcage.

Being a vertebrate means you have a backbone.

If you run fast, your pulse rate will increase.

Pulse rate measures how fast the heart is beating.

It's very important to make sure you do regular exercise.

Muscles need a supply of oxygen to function.

Many other animals, called invertebrates, have an external shell.

The skeleton protects the organs inside your body.

Oxygen is carried in the blood from the lungs to the muscles.

© Copyright HeadStart Primary Ltd 2016

PUMPKINS

The left-hand column lists a number of **main** ideas about pumpkins. The right-hand column presents a list of **details**. Draw lines matching up each **main idea** with the appropriate **detail**.

A pumpkin is a member of the squash family of plants with a thick yellow or orange skin.	Lanterns were originally carved from turnips in Ireland and taken to the USA by emigrants.
Pumpkins are a native plant of America. Evidence of the earliest pumpkin seeds comes from Mexico.	Pumpkins, a versatile ingredient in many recipes, are also a very good source of vitamins.
Pumpkins grown for human consumption are very nutritious and high in fibre.	Its thick, protective skin contains edible pulp and the seeds necessary for future pumpkins.
Carving pumpkins into Jack o' Lanterns is a tradition that goes back hundreds of years.	When watering try to keep the leaves and fruit dry as this can lead to rot.
Pumpkin seeds should be planted at the end of May and harvested in October.	Whatever their origin, pumpkins are now grown all over the world apart from Antarctica.
Growing pumpkins are very thirsty plants and need a lot of water especially during dry weather.	Good seed is important. If seeds are stored properly, they can be saved for several years.

Inferences

Strand: Making inferences

National Curriculum reference:

- drawing inferences such as inferring characters' feelings, thoughts and motives from their actions

Reading Test / Content Domain links: 2a, 2b, 2d, 2f, 2g

LEGENDARY LIVES

Here are a number of legendary characters. Try to guess who or what they are from their own descriptions.

Occupation: outlaw
Outfit: Lincoln green
Hobbies: archery, being merry, and robbing the rich to give to the poor.

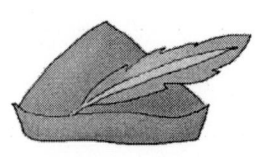

Occupation: magician
Residence: bottles and lamps
Hobbies: granting wishes, doing a few tricks when summoned and appearing in a puff of smoke.

Occupation: unemployed
Outfit: tail of a fish
Hobbies: sitting on rocks, combing hair and luring sailors to their deaths now and again.

Occupation: cleaner
Outfit: rags and glass slippers
Hobbies: dancing, dreaming of a better life without my horrid sisters and marrying a prince.

Occupation: dental assistant
Outfit: frills, wings, wand
Hobbies: collecting teeth from under pillows and leaving cash to help with purchase of toothpaste.

Occupation: big brute
Outfit: hairy and usually white
Hobbies: surprising the people who live in the Himalayas, especially visitors who think I don't exist.

ON THE PHONE

If you overheard someone on their phone, would you be able to guess who they were talking to? They might be speaking to a member of the family, a doctor or a friend. Use the clues available to decide who is on the other end of the phone.

WHO?

Who else is going? What time? How much is it? Ok. I'll see what Mum and Dad say and let you know tomorrow at school.

_____

I don't know. We were out for the evening. Between 7pm and 11pm, I suppose. Yes, the doors were locked. Broken glass everywhere.

_____

We've tried everything. The picture keeps disappearing or else it says: 'no signal'. Yes, I'll be in on Friday. What time on Friday?

_____

Spots all over. He was fine yesterday. I'm taking him to the doctor in an hour. Yes, I'll come and get any homework this afternoon.

_____

Oh, probably three months ago. Yes, they're absolutely filthy. Can hardly see out of them. Do you clean inside as well as outside?

_____

WHO?

She doesn't look well at all. She hasn't moved from her chair and that's not like her. Eyes are glazed over. Oh... she's not wagging her tail.

_____

Can you be here at 6:30am? There are six of us. Yes, 65 East Street. Where to? The airport. Two suitcases and four small bags. Thanks.

_____

Andy's going and some of my other friends from class. Yes, I promise, and I'll do the washing-up all week. Really? Great!

_____

Do you think it's serious? My next-door neighbour says there's a lot of it about. Two tablets every four hours? I'll do that.

_____

Can I collect it on Saturday? Yes, marzipan and icing, but definitely no nuts. Ten candles – that's right. The party's in the afternoon.

_____

GRANDPA AND A CAT CALLED ALICE

Here is a story in which you have to work some things out for yourself.

SARDINES FOR ALICE

My grandpa has a cat called Alice. Funny that. My grandma was called Alice. In fact, the cat used to be called Kitty, but now it's Alice.

There's a lot of funny things about Grandpa. When I go to see him, the front door is always open. The TV is on. The cat is usually on top of the TV or the kitchen table, eating last week's cake. Grandpa will say it was lovely cake, even though he hasn't eaten any. He never says it was delicious, though I tell Mum that's what he said.

I go out into the back garden. Flower scent, deckchair, buzzing bees, and grass that needs cutting. At the far end is the shed where Grandpa will be humming a tune to himself. Knock on the door... and here he is.

"Hello, Grandpa. You all right?"

"Hello, Tommy. Yes. Looks like I'm still here. Oh, that was a lovely cake you brought last week. A real smasher. Say thanks to your mum."

It's cosy in his shed. Some of his drawings are pinned to the wall. Some photographs of him with Grandma. Some of the cat. And loads of tubes of paint everywhere, paintbrushes, empty jam jars and oily rags. I love the smell. Paint is all over his hands or drying on his trousers. He doesn't care. He doesn't care that the front door is open. Not now that he's on his own. He's painting a picture of Alice among the flowers.

"Secretive, isn't she? There and not there. Now, she'll always be there waiting for sardines."

"Not so secretive when she's sitting on the television."

"Hah!" says Grandpa, ruffling my hair and shaking with laughter.

1. Whose grandma was called Alice?
   _____

2. Why does the narrator use the word 'was' when he says: "My grandma **was** called Alice"?
   _____

3. Why do you think Grandpa has changed the cat's name?
   _____

4. Why does Grandpa never say the cake was delicious?
   _____

5. Why do you think the narrator always tells his mum that Grandpa said the cake was delicious?
   _____
   _____

6. What time of year do you think it is?
   _____

7. How do you know? Write down one piece of evidence.
   _____

8. What evidence is there to suggest that Grandpa is happy working in his shed?
   _____

9. Write down **three** things that tell you Grandpa is an artist.
   _____
   _____
   _____

10. How do you know Grandpa enjoys Tommy's visits?
    _____

© Copyright HeadStart Primary Ltd 2016

GRANDPA AND A CAT CALLED ALICE   part 2

Read what happens next and answer the questions. Again, you'll have to use your skills at 'reading between the lines'.

Mum is in the kitchen, staring out of the window. I ask her if she is baking a cake for Grandpa, because he always says how delicious they are.

Holding my face, she says she won't be making a cake. There won't be any more cakes. At first, I don't understand. Then I realise. I stand beside her staring out of the window.

On my way to Grandpa's house, I buy a tin of sardines at the shop at the end of Grandpa's street. The woman who owns the shop smiles and won't take any money from me.

Grandpa's door is closed, but he always kept a spare key under the mat. The TV is switched off. Alice is sitting on the kitchen table and rubs her head against my hands as I scoop sardines into her bowl.

Outside, the grass still needs cutting. The bees buzz around a deckchair, empty apart from an old straw hat.

As I open the shed door, I feel a lump in my throat and an ache in my chest. Inside, it doesn't feel as cosy as it usually does. Brushes and tubes of paint are everywhere. Grandpa has pinned a photograph of himself next to the one of Grandma. On his table, leaning against the wall, is a new painting. The colours are brilliant. It's a painting of the garden and the deckchair, and, sitting in the deckchair, is Grandpa in his straw hat.

There's a note beside it. It says: "This is for you, Tommy. Now, I'll always be there, waiting for delicious cake."

Outside, I pick up the hat and sit in the deckchair. I read the note again and smile at Grandpa's joke.

© Copyright HeadStart Primary Ltd 2016

1. What do you think Mum is doing while staring out of the window? **Circle one.**

   | looking at the garden | thinking about Grandpa | watching the rain |

2. Why do you think she holds Tommy's face?
   _____

3. Tommy says, "Then I realise." What does he realise?
   _____

4. Why does the shop-owner give Tommy the sardines for free?
   _____

5. Describe **two** things that are different when Tommy arrives at Grandpa's house this time.
   _____
   _____

6. How is Tommy feeling as he stands at the shed door and how do you know?
   _____
   _____

7. Why do you think Grandpa has pinned a photograph of himself next to the one of Grandma?
   _____

8. The note says: 'I'll always be there.' What does Grandpa mean?
   _____
   _____

9. Read the last sentence again. What is Grandpa's joke?
   _____
   _____

© Copyright HeadStart Primary Ltd 2016

Justifying inferences with evidence

Strand: Making inferences

National Curriculum reference:

- drawing inferences such as inferring characters' feelings, thoughts and motives from their actions, and justifying inferences with evidence

Reading Test / Content Domain links: 2a, 2b, 2d, 2f, 2g

BODY LANGUAGE

Read the following two scenes. If you had been walking by and had seen these events, would you be able to guess at what was going on?

Molly's grandad stood in front of the cash machine, searching his pockets. He scratched his head and smiled at Molly. He searched his pockets again. He looked on the ground at his feet. "Don't worry, Molly," he said, checking his watch. "We're ahead of schedule." Lowering her swimming kit onto the ground, Molly sighed as a bus turned the corner and raced by without stopping.

1. What had Molly's grandad lost?

    _____

2. How do you know?

    _____
    _____

3. Why does he smile at Molly?

    _____

4. What makes you think that?

    _____

5. Why does he check his watch?

    _____

6. Why does Molly sigh?

    _____

7. Where do you think they were going?

    _____

Mr and Mrs Jeffreys sat in their dressing gowns peering through a gap in the living room curtains. Mr Jeffreys didn't, for a moment, take his eyes off the flower beds in the front garden, as he put his empty cereal bowl on the table. Four empty cups of coffee already sat there.

"Not long now," whispered Mrs Jeffreys as the sun came up. "I suppose I could have rung the neighbour's doorbell." Mr Jeffreys scowled.

The living room clock chimed seven when Champ jumped over the wall. Immediately, Mr Jeffreys ran out, waving his arms and hollering, causing it to panic and drop its bone as it ran off.

1. What time of day is it?

   _____

2. How do you know?

   _____
   _____

3. Have Mr and Mrs Jeffreys been sitting there for some time?

   _____

4. How do you know?

   _____

5. How does Mrs Jeffreys feel about being there?

   _____

6. Who is Champ?

   _____

7. Why does Mr Jeffreys rush out of the house waving his arms and hollering?

   _____
   _____

FIRST WOMAN IN SPACE

Read this short biography of how Valentina Tereshkova came to be the first woman in space, then answer the questions that follow.

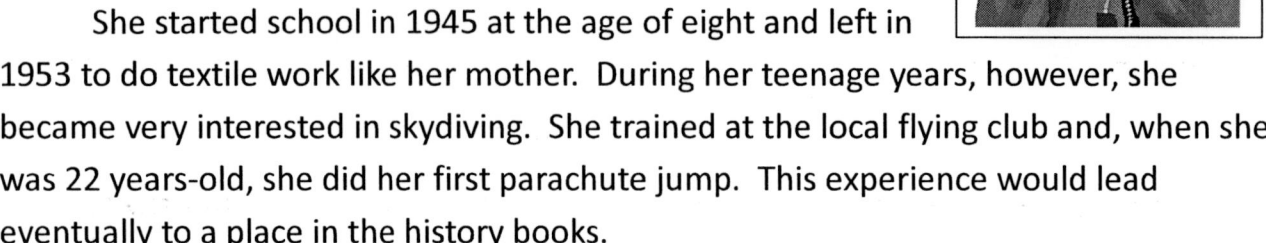

Valentina Tereshkova was born in 1937 in a small village in central Russia, where her father was a tractor driver and her mother worked in a textile factory.

She started school in 1945 at the age of eight and left in 1953 to do textile work like her mother. During her teenage years, however, she became very interested in skydiving. She trained at the local flying club and, when she was 22 years-old, she did her first parachute jump. This experience would lead eventually to a place in the history books.

Her enthusiasm for skydiving brought her to the attention of the country's Space Programme. Russia had already put the first man into space in 1961, when Yuri Gagarin orbited the Earth. The government was very eager to achieve another Russian 'first' in what was known as the *space race* against the USA.

In fact, a Russian newspaper at the time reported that Tereshkova had 'dreamt of going into space' as soon as she heard about Gagarin's space mission.

Her dream and her skydiving abilities made her a likely candidate for the intensive training necessary to become an astronaut. Her training included weightless flights at high altitudes, isolation tests and spacecraft engineering. Skill in handling a parachute was an essential part of re-entry. Whoever was chosen would have to be ejected from the space capsule at 20,000 feet and land safely. She was selected in February 1962.

On the morning of 16th June 1963, Tereshkova was bussed to the launch pad. After routine communication and life support checks, she was sealed inside the rocket, Vostok 6. There followed a two-hour countdown and a successful launch.

She completed 48 orbits of the Earth in 71 hours – more time in space than all the American astronauts combined.

Back on Earth she was highly honoured, not only in her own country, where she received the Hero of the Soviet Union medal, but also around the world.

She never went into space again, but perhaps her spirit of adventure did not leave her. In 2013, she said she'd be happy to go on a one-way trip to Mars.

© Copyright HeadStart Primary Ltd 2016

Now use evidence from the text to answer the following questions.

1. Do you think Valentina's parents expected her to grow up to be a famous astronaut? Why do you think this?

   _____
   _____

2. Why were her skydiving skills so important?

   _____
   _____

3. How do we know that Yuri Gagarin's space flight was a factor in Tereshkova's desire to be part of the Space Programme?

   _____

4. During her training for space travel, she had to have 'isolation tests'. Why do you think this would be part of the training?

   _____
   _____

5. Re-entry involved being 'ejected at 20,000 feet'. What does **ejected** mean?

   _____

6. It might be fair to say that, at this point in history, Russia was winning the *space race* against the USA. Give **two** reasons why it is fair to say this.

   _____
   _____

7. From what is said in the text, how do we know she became world-famous?

   _____

8. Did she ever lose her spirit of adventure? How do you know?

   _____
   _____

© Copyright HeadStart Primary Ltd 2016

Predicting what might happen

Strand: Making inferences

National Curriculum reference:

- predicting what might happen from details stated and implied

Reading Test / Content Domain links: 2a, 2b, 2e

WHAT'S NEXT?

Read these incomplete sentences. Write down what you think happened next.

1. I had always thought that holidays were exciting, until _____
   _____

2. Although I knew the castle wasn't haunted, when I opened the door, _____
   _____

3. Aunt Jemima drove off into the mist in her battered, old car and _____
   _____

4. As the sun came up, I stuck my head out of the tent and saw _____
   _____
   _____

5. When Uncle Rashid said he had a mythical creature in his shed, we _____
   _____

6. Unwrapping the present from my cousin, Marty the Magician, I found _____
   _____

7. A terrifying roar told us the lions had escaped, so we _____
   _____

8. The detective, with all the evidence he needed, looked round the room and pointed at _____
   _____

9. In the middle of the night, my cat wandered into my bedroom and _____
   _____

© Copyright HeadStart Primary Ltd 2016

HOW DO THINGS TURN OUT?

Here are some short descriptions of events. Decide what happens in the end.

The snow had stayed for a whole week without any sign of it melting. Kim and Sanjay spent every breaktime at school working on their snowman. Kim had even brought in an old scarf and hat. They were just adding the final touches: an upturned arc for a smile, when...

_____
_____
_____

Dad said the south coast was a great place to look for fossils. So we all piled into the car, including our dog, Suzi. My bag was bursting with fossil books, my fossil-hunter's hammer, sketch book, pencils and magnifying glass. So it was a pity we spent all day finding absolutely nothing. At dusk, dejected, we trailed back to the car. That's when Suzi came over wagging her tail.

_____
_____
_____

Class 5 organised a cake sale for charity. We must have made hundreds of cakes. I don't think anybody counted them all. Our headteacher let us sell them at breaktime and after lunch. When we finished, we had nearly £60 for Save The Children and we still had quite a lot of cakes left over, so this is what we did.

_____
_____
_____

© Copyright HeadStart Primary Ltd 2016

PETS AND PESTS

Here are some scenes involving pets. Using the clues provided, write down what you think might happen next.

> Aditya was so pleased with the amazing cake he baked at school that he couldn't wait to see his mum's face. To avoid spoiling the cherries decorating the top and getting dollops of cream all over his shirt, he pushed the door open with his elbow.
> At that moment, Sparky, his lively Beagle, its tongue dangling and ears flapping as if he were about to take flight, came racing towards him.
>
> _____
> _____
> _____

> Every weekend, it was Maggie's job to feed the cat. She'd become so used to cleaning Mitzi's water dish and filling up her food bowl with cat food, she could almost do it with her eyes closed.
> This particular weekend, it looked as if Dad had brought some fish home for Mitzi as a special treat. The cat certainly scoffed it all pretty quickly. When Dad went in the kitchen to cook some home-made fish and chips, he came out looking a bit puzzled.
>
> _____
> _____
> _____

> Charlie loved snakes. All snakes. Well, not those with deadly poison, or the ones that squeezed you to bits. The trouble was keeping an eye on them. They were very sneaky – all seven of them.
> Unfortunately, his Aunt Betty and Uncle Maynard, who had just arrived for tea, weren't so keen on reptiles of any sort. Charlie counted his snakes: "... and that makes six..."
>
> _____
> _____
> _____
> _____

WHAT IF?

What would happen if fairytales didn't go according to plan? Here are some reminders of some well-known fairytale scenes, but with an unexpected twist. Write down what you think might happen next.

Cinderella wished she could go to the ball too, like her ugly sisters. Suddenly, there was a whoosh! Her fairy godmother fell out of a tree and bent her wand. When she tried to use it to magically transform four white mice into four magnificent horses to pull Cinderella's golden carriage,...

_____
_____
_____

The seven dwarves were so happy to have Snow White stay in their cottage in the heart of the forest. Their rooms were always an untidy mess. The next day, they went off to work whistling and returned in the evening with a spring in their step, expecting to find the place spotless and sparkling. The trouble was Snow White wasn't any use at domestic chores. As soon as they opened the door...

_____
_____
_____

The three bears were about to have their porridge, when Mummy Bear suggested they go for a walk first to let it cool down. Daddy Bear agreed. Baby Bear loved to go for walks, so off they went. Meanwhile, Goldilocks, smelling the delicious porridge, sneaked into the house and was delighted to find no one there. No one, that is, apart from grumpy, old Grandpa Bear, who...

_____
_____
_____

Jack raced across the landscape of clouds where the giant lived. Even with the hen that laid golden eggs under his arm, he knew he could reach the top of the beanstalk before the lumbering giant caught him. Clambering down to the bottom, he immediately grabbed his axe and began hacking away at the beanstalk. If only he had sharpened the axe, he might have…

_____
_____
_____

Little Red Riding Hood was skipping through the dark woods when Mr Wolf stepped out of the shadows. He was a cunning character, not to be trusted for a minute. Unfortunately, Little Red Riding Hood was a very helpful, chatty girl. Not only did she mention she was on her way to her grandma's house, she gave Mr Wolf directions how to get there. He gave a wicked snarl, showing his sharp teeth and raced off ahead of her. The trouble was Red Riding Hood had a very poor sense of direction. By mistake, she sent him to the woodcutter's cottage, where…

_____
_____
_____

As the three pigs began to build their house, the Big Bad Wolf watched from his hiding place at the edge of the woods. One of the pigs already had a barrow-load of bricks. Another had piled up some heavy wooden beams. The third pig, however, had made do with some straw. As night approached, the Big Bad Wolf stood outside the house of straw and huffed and puffed till he blew the house down. This particular pig had no building skills whatsoever, except that he'd been training at the gym recently – mainly body-building. So when the Big Bad Wolf…

_____
_____
_____

Features of texts

Strand: Comprehension / Themes and Conventions

National Curriculum reference:

- identifying how language, structure and presentation contribute to meaning
- identifying themes and conventions in a wide range of books

Reading Test / Content Domain links: 2a, 2b, 2f, 2g

A MOVING TOY

This text about a moving toy is missing a title and subheadings. Many of the features that are there, however, should help you to decide what kind of text it is. Answer the questions that follow.

TITLE: _____

A _____

cardboard box about the size of a packet of tea

coloured card

dowel

cardboard discs

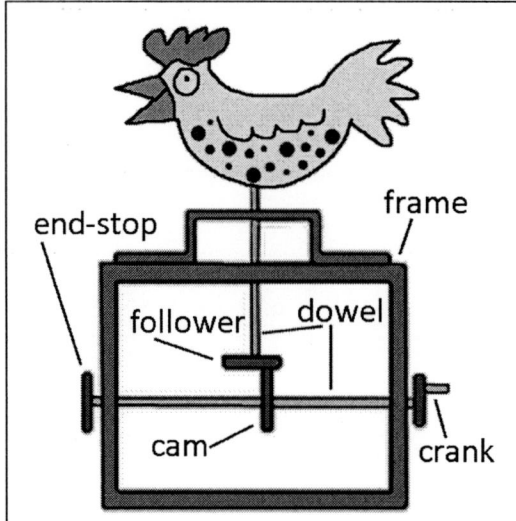

B _____

scissors, craft knife, cutting board and hole punch, saw, glue

coloured pens or paint and brushes

C _____

1. Glue together 3 cardboard discs for the cam, 3 discs for the follower, 2 discs for the crank and 2 discs for the end-stop.
2. Find the centre of the top of the box and punch a hole just big enough for the dowel. Do the same on 2 sides of the box.
3. Glue an extra, folded piece of card to the top of the box with a central hole. Align its hole with hole in top of box.
4. Push piece of dowel through side of box, fit and glue cam in the middle before pushing dowel through other side. Fit end-stop.
5. Repeat same procedure with vertical dowel and follower.
6. Glue on crank and add creature of choice.
7. When glue is dry, turn handle.

D _____

Never walk around with sharp tools. Be aware of other children working.

E _____

cam – disc that creates movement.
dowel – thin wooden rod.
follower – part that is moved by a cam.
frame – structure that contains moving parts.
crank – handle that turns the cam.
end-stop – keeps dowel in position.

1. Think of a title and write it here.

   _____

2. Think up appropriate sub-headings for the following sections:

   A _____

   B _____

   C _____

   D _____

   E _____

3. Write down **three** examples of imperative verbs.

   _____

   _____

   _____

4. In section **B**, why do you think some items have been kept separate from the others?

   _____

   _____

5. Why does section **C** contain numbers?

   _____

6. Looking at the diagram, which part doesn't move?

   _____

7. What kind of text is this?

   _____

FEATURES OF FABLES

Here is one of Aesop's fables – The Ant and the Dove. Check it for the usual features of fables, then complete the table below.

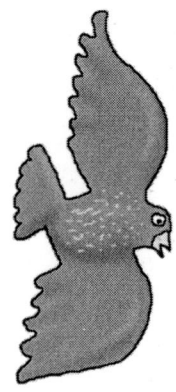

The Ant and the Dove

One day, when the sun was fiercely hot, an ant trudged his way to the stream to quench his thirst. Being small and quite exhausted by the heat, he tumbled into the water. Pushed this way and pulled that way by the strong current, he was on the point of drowning. A dove, nesting on a branch overhanging the stream, witnessed the ant's predicament.

Quickly, she plucked a nearby leaf and let it float down close to the ant, who, with a final exertion, was able to scramble onto it and float to safety. "I won't forget your kindness," said the ant.

Some days later, a bird-catcher, impressed by the song of the dove, arrived to set a trap of lime twigs for the bird. He knew which berries it found irresistible.

The ant, realising his intention, stung him in the foot. Limping in pain, the bird-catcher made such a howling noise, the dove took flight.

[The moral of this story is that one good turn deserves another.]

feature	evidence
opening lacks detail	
animal characters	
example of animal speaking	
unrealistic plot	
simple setting	
limited sketch of a character	
a lesson about life	

THE TEAMS

Here are two accounts of the same event. As you read them, notice how they describe the same experience in different ways.

LAST GIRL STANDING

SCENE: School playing field. Nineteen girls are standing in front of the supply teacher, who has a box of hockey sticks beside her. It's a dull day.

———————————

CAST: Mrs Reid - a supply teacher.
Ruth, Lucy and Mara – Year 5 pupils.

———————————

Mrs Reid: *(looking at the sky)* Come on, girls, let's get on with it before the rain starts. Lucy, you and Mara pick the teams.
Ruth: *(head drooping)* Not again.
Mrs Reid: What was that, Ruth?
Ruth: Nothing, Miss.
Lucy: *(smiling at her best friend, Carla)* I pick Carla.
Mara: *(pointing at Leila who is jumping up and down)* I'll have Leila.
Ruth: *(mimicking Mara)* I'll have Leila.
Mrs Reid: Ruth, please be quiet.

(Ruth stands staring at the ground as the teams are chosen. The teams have equal numbers and Ruth has not been picked.)

Mrs Reid: *(feeling sorry for Ruth)* Don't worry, Ruth, you can join Lucy's team.
Mara: *(frowning)* But that would be unfair, Miss!
Lucy: Well, I don't mind if Mara has her.
Mara: I didn't say I wanted her.
Mrs Reid: Thank you, girls, but I'll sort this out. Come and choose your hockey sticks. We'll start the match in a minute.
Ruth: *(shakes her head and wanders back to her class)* Don't worry, Miss. It's always like this. Every Tuesday. They never pick me.
Mrs Reid: Ruth! Ruth!

<u>Monday night</u> –

Supply teacher again tomorrow. Fingers crossed, she sorts out the teams herself, or else it rains. Don't want to be last one standing again. Embarrassing!!! Not so bad when Gabby's with me, but she's got a cold or something. Lucky her.

<u>Tuesday evening</u> –

Well, that's it for another week. Just as I expected. Mrs Reid's all right. I thought she was going to choose the teams herself, but changed her mind. Maybe I'll catch Gabby's cold in time for games next week, if I try hard enough.

1. What sort of text is **Last Girl Standing**?

   _____

2. In **Last Girl Standing**, what do the first three sentences describe?

   _____

3. What does **CAST** refer to?

   _____

4. Write down an example of stage directions.

   _____

5. One set of stage directions describes Leila jumping up and down. Why do you think she was doing that?

   _____

6. Do you think Lucy and Mara are picking the best teams or their best friends?

   _____

7. What kind of text is the one that begins **Monday night**?

   _____

8. How do you know it's this kind of text?

   _____

9. Why might Ruth want the supply teacher to sort out the teams?

   _____

11. Which text is better at showing you what Ruth is thinking? Why do you think this?

    _____ because _____

    _____

    _____

Features of texts and meaning

Strand: Comprehension / Themes and Conventions

National Curriculum reference:

- identifying how language, structure and presentation contribute to meaning
- recognising some different forms of poetry
- identifying themes and conventions in a wide range of books

Reading Test / Content Domain links: 2a, 2b, 2f, 2g

LOCAL NEWS REPORT

Here is a report in a local newspaper. Think about the features you expect in a news item and answer the questions.

CATWOMAN CAUSES CHAOS

Known locally as the Catwoman, 89-year-old Kitty Parker of Albee Avenue, received a visit today from PC D. Zaster, following a complaint from neighbours.

Kitty, a kindly woman and a frequent sight at the Church bingo sessions, is the proud owner of thirty-nine cats. For many years, she has been giving a home to any stray cat that turns up on her doorstep. This generosity of spirit isn't normally a problem for her neighbours, except when there is a full moon.

"Once a month," stated Evan Knowes, who lives opposite Mrs Parker, "the cats all line up along the garden wall and wail their heads off. I've had enough. I have to get up early to go to work and this is unacceptable."

Another neighbour, who didn't want to give her name, told our reporter that the caterwauling had put her dog off its biscuits. She said that when the howling starts up, Squiffy her Pekinese goes flying into its basket as if it were catapulted there.

A spokesman from the RSPCA confirmed that an officer from their organisation had recently inspected the house and was reassured to find that all the cats were well looked after and in good health. The RSPCA spokeswoman was not prepared to say how tunefully they sang.

Mrs Parker told us that she never hears them, possibly because she is a little deaf and doesn't always hear the numbers being called at bingo. She also insisted that, despite a number of claims on social media, at no time has she joined her cats in singing the chorus.

PC Zaster pointed out that the cat-calling falls into a very minor category of public nuisance. No further actions will be taken against Mrs Parker. He has also assured local residents that everything is now under control. Once a month, when the moon is full, he will stand guard by the cat flap to prevent a repeat of this incident.

<u>Breaking news</u>
Late last night, we heard from Kitty Parker that several of her cats have had kittens. This brings the total number of her feline companions to ninety-six. Anyone who might like to own a kitten should contact her in Albee Avenue.

1. How does the 1st paragraph answer the following questions?

   Who? _____

   What has happened? _____

   Where? _____

2. What does the article tell us about Kitty Parker?

   _____

   _____

   _____

3. Describe the incident that neighbours have complained about.

   _____

   _____

4. Four other people are mentioned in this report. Who are they?

   _____

   _____

5. Write down an example of direct speech.

   _____

   _____

6. Write down an example of indirect speech.

   _____

   _____

7. The newspaper article has two concluding statements. What are they?

   _____

   _____

   _____

PLASTIC BAGS

Plastic carrier bags are a common sight when you're out shopping. Here are some facts about how they are produced and then used.

Introduction: The Life Cycle of the Plastic Bag
Ever since their invention in the 1930s, every year, trillions of plastic carrier bags have been produced and given to shoppers. They are used, on average, for 20 minutes before being thrown away and left to pollute our planet for hundreds of years.

Production
The raw ingredient of your plastic bag is oil. This is heated to produce a gas, which is then converted into granules. These are heated, stretched and cooled to make bags. The main manufacturing countries are China, India and Thailand.

Transport
After coloured inks are added and they are printed with supermarket logos, they are shipped to Britain. The distance they travel by ship and by truck, from where they are made to our local shops and stores, can be as much as 8000 miles.

Advantages
They are strong (most can hold 10 kg or more of shopping), compact and cheap: one plastic bag costs as little as 0.5p to make and deliver.

Use
A third of shoppers re-use them for bin-liners, and another third re-use them for shopping, but, in the end, 98% end up in landfill, whereas about 200 million litter the countryside.

Decay
Plastic bags haven't been around long enough for us to know how long they can last. Scientists estimate it may take more than 400 years for them to disintegrate. Chemicals in the printing inks can pollute the land, including farmland. Plastic bags in the sea can survive unchanged for a very long time. Every year, plastic bags floating in the oceans contribute to the deaths of a million seabirds and 100,000 whales, seals and turtles every year. Unfortunately, once the creature's body has decayed, the plastic will remain to kill again.

1. Write down **three** important phrases in the **Introduction** that tell the reader what this is all about.

   _____

   _____

   _____

2. Write down **two** technical phrases used in the description of how bags are produced.

   _____

   _____

3. What links the information in the two arrow-shaped boxes?

   _____

4. The **Advantages** box tries to answer the question **Why**. How does it do that?

   _____

   _____

5. Give **two** examples of numbers or statistics being used to describe the size of the problem.

   _____

   _____

6. How might farmland be affected?

   _____

7. How does the **Introduction** relate to the last section called **Decay**?

   _____

   _____

   _____

© Copyright HeadStart Primary Ltd 2016

ROBOTS: A BALANCED VIEW

Harry is presenting a balanced argument to his class about the pros and cons of robots and artificial intelligence.

My group has put together this talk. I'm going to argue that new stuff happening in what's called artificial intelligence is the most amazing, exciting thing going on right now. We're all used to the idea of robotic arms working in car assembly lines, but the next step is to go beyond this and create intelligent machines.

There are different points of view. Scientists don't agree about whether robots can ever really be intelligent or not. Whereas some say that we're on the brink of producing artificially intelligent machines; others argue that we don't properly understand how human intelligence works. It's not the same as programming a computer.

Sometime in the future, I, personally, believe we will have smart machines that can learn new things, solve problems and work things out for themselves without having to be programmed by a human being. We've had chess-playing computers for a long time now. But new robots will be able to learn new games and chat while you're playing.

In my opinion, one day, robots will do lots of the boring jobs, so that people don't have to do them. You must agree that this is a good thing. Isn't it also better to have clever machines doing some of the dangerous work that people risk their lives doing? They will work accurately and never get tired or ill.

Finally, some people worry that we'll be dominated by mad, terminator machines. What, I believe, scientists will never be able to do is create a thinking robot that feels things like anger, sadness or happiness. Machines are machines and we will be in charge. This isn't the movies.

© Copyright HeadStart Primary Ltd 2016

1. Write down the sentence that Harry uses to introduce his topic.

   _____

2. Give **three** examples of the kinds of words and phrases you commonly find in balanced arguments.

   _____

   _____

3. Harry expresses his personal opinion now and again in order to be persuasive. Write down **two** examples.

   _____

   _____

4. Harry argues that intelligent robots will be smarter than any machine invented so far. What does he compare them to?

   _____

5. He does admit that scientists still have a long way to go. What is the main problem they face?

   _____

6. Harry suggests that there are advantages in having robots doing jobs that human beings do at the moment. What are these advantages?

   _____

   _____

7. Harry believes that we shouldn't be frightened of the idea of intelligent robots. What does he say in his conclusion to reassure us?

   _____

   _____

Words that capture the reader's imagination

Strand: Language for effect

National Curriculum reference:

- discussing words and phrases that capture the reader's interest and imagination

Reading Test / Content Domain links: 2a, 2b, 2g

LOOK AT THE MOON

Here is a poem about the moon comparing it to different things, using a mixture of metaphors and similes. After you've read it, decide whether the things it's compared to are metaphors or similes. Then **tick** the correct boxes.

MOON

Moon is a crumpled handkerchief
A flag of quiet surrender unfurled
It's like the face of the planetary clock
Tick-tocking its way around the world
Sometimes it's like the farmer's scythe
Levelling the ready corn
Or like a silver bottle top – a medal never worn
The moon is a sailboat circumnavigating the Earth
As fast as a homing bird racing for all its worth
The finger of wisdom pointing to the answer
As bent as an old man – as straight as a dancer
Like the smile of a cat, the moon is a mystery
A story of watchers and rhymers from history
It flies like a silver discus thrown by a giant
Striding across the velvet sky dark and defiant
The perfect birdwing on a summer evening
So silent in its flight
A surprise guest in the morning
But like a constant
friend of night

Now decide whether the words and phrases in the table are part of a metaphor or a simile and put a **tick** in the correct box. Do you remember the difference between a simile and metaphor?

word or phrase	metaphor	simile
crumpled handkerchief		
flag of quiet surrender		
face of the planetary clock		
farmer's scythe		
silver bottle top		
medal		
sailboat		
homing bird		
finger of wisdom		
old man		
dancer		
smile of a cat		
mystery		
story of watchers and rhymers		
silver discus		
perfect birdwing		
surprise guest		
constant companion		

WHERE DO SUPERHEROES SHOP?

Here is a window display of items a superhero might need or be persuaded to buy. Look out for the persuasive techniques being used.

SUPERSTUFF

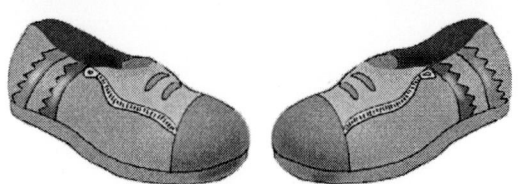

Toe-tingling trainers to make eyes turn and set tongues wagging. Luminous side strips to avoid putting a foot wrong in the dark. Remote-control zippers essential for fast getaways. Totally water- and zap-proof. Buy one, get the other one free!

We call it the Visibility Cloak, because you'll want people in the street to see you strut around in this all-weather, flight-guaranteed, one-size-fits-all superhero requirement. Thought-activated speed control comes as standard.

Our unique range of superhero, bullet-proof t-shirts come in a variety of outrageous colours, with extra padding for clients who still need to visit the gym. A range of heroic logos available.

A miracle of technology, the Big League Bad-Guy Beater is a belt for all those necessary gizmos no self-respecting superhero can be without. Pockets for lasers, thought-readers and snacks.

Secret Identity Masks. Do you want to be caught out being Mr or Mrs Ordinary? Do you want to be spotted at the check-out? Instead, why don't you check out our extraordinary visors and veils? Wearing one is like pulling on pure greatness.

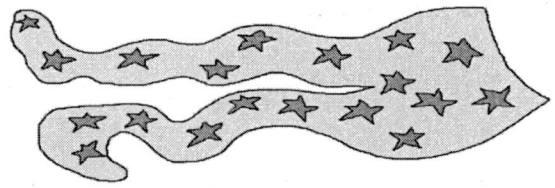

Superstuff's Supertights are a must for those interplanetary trips to the colder corners of the universe, or even a quick hop to the dark side of the moon. These chill-breakers come with spangles, stars or lightning flashes.

1. Write down **two** examples of alliteration.

   _____

   _____

2. What word is used to suggest that the t-shirts are like no others?

   _____

3. Write down **two** examples of words or phrases that are meant to sound scientific.

   _____

   _____

4. Find **two** examples of questions designed to engage the reader.

   _____

   _____

5. Write down an example of a simile.

   _____

6. **Two** phrases are used which claim the trainers and the belt are absolutely necessary if you want to look like a superhero. What are they?

   _____

   _____

7. If you wanted to impress people which **two** items do they suggest you buy?

   _____

8. What superhero activities might the Supertights help with?

   _____

   _____

BLOCKBUSTER

Here is a review of the latest summer blockbuster film. Some of the language is 'over the top' in the hope that you will be persuaded to go and see it. Write down all the similes and metaphors you can find and some of the more interesting adjectives.

THE REVIEW

It's aliens versus the robot dinosaurs in this must-see, big-budget mammoth of a blockbuster: Dinotron Uprising.

Set in a fantasy future, where the entire human population has skipped off to Mars to leave it to our mechanical, freaky friends, the Dinotrons – like a car park of heaving, scaly, self-drive reptiles – to protect the Earth from the muscle-bound, makers of mayhem, the Zameleons.

The trouble began when, still inhabiting the home planet, we let the compulsory bad guy – a temper tantrum in a hat and ill-fitting moustache – set up a zoo for inter-planetary aliens. Cue the careless zookeeper and you have sloppiness-on-a-stick forgetting to lock up properly. For a while, the shape-shifting Zameleons behave like a bunch of rather disgruntled shoppers. If that weren't scary enough, they soon get grumpier and capture our wise-cracking hero, Chuck.

Bring on the Dinotrons. Being eaten by a metal T Rex is like jumping into the shredder, so don't try this at home. Of course, the word, "Run!" is not part of their programming.

The stage is set for the ultimate confrontation. We can only hope and pray that either a Dinotron or a Zameleon eats Chuck before he inflicts any more of his awful jokes on us.

Adjectives

_____

_____

_____

_____

_____

_____

_____

_____

_____

_____

_____

_____

_____

_____

_____

_____

Similes

_____

_____

_____

_____

_____

Metaphors

_____

_____

_____

_____

_____

A ROLLERCOASTER OF PERSUASION

Here is an ad for a theme park. Look at the persuasive language being used and answer the questions that follow.

A warm welcome awaits you at WONDERPARK!

Are you ready for a day of action-filled adventure – a day like no other?

If you've bought a discounted family ticket (including free car parking), then you are already half-way to a journey through the raging, rollicking rapids of Pirateland. Check out the once-in-a-lifetime thrill of the Dinosaur Jungle. (Don't forget your running shoes!) Or, if you are bold enough, you might prefer the waking nightmare that is the Intergalactic Death Cruise. Our dreamilicious, magical Fantasy Zone is like all your birthdays happening at once.

If rollercoasters are not your thing, come and get splat-happy in one of our games arcades.

(With 10 restaurants and cafes, we can cater to all your needs. A meal for a family of four is included in your ticket.)

IT'S WEIRD... IT'S WACKY... IT'S WONDERPARK!

1. Find **two** examples of alliteration.

_____

_____

2. Twice, the ad points out what good value a ticket is. Write down **both** examples.

_____

_____

3. Sometimes questions are used to engage the reader. Write down an example.
   _____

4. Find the writer's attempt to include a joke.
   _____

5. Write down the phrase that sounds like a dare or a challenge.
   _____

6. Write down an example of a metaphor being used.
   _____

7. Write down an example of a simile.
   _____

8. The writer uses **two** phrases that suggest your day at Wonderpark will be unique. What are they?
   _____
   _____

9. Write down **two** made-up words.
   _____   _____

10. Write down an example of a slogan.
    _____

11. What pronoun does the writer use throughout the text to give the impression he is speaking personally to the reader?
    _____

12. Write down a word or phrase that would persuade you to buy a ticket.
    _____

Explaining how words and phrases enhance meaning

Strand: Language for effect

National Curriculum reference:

- discussing words and phrases that capture the reader's interest and imagination

Reading Test / Content Domain links: 2a, 2b, 2g

WHAT IS THE AUTHOR UP TO?

Choosing the right words is very important. You might be trying to give clear information, make people stop and think, persuade the reader to do something or entertain them. In the next four pages, what are the authors trying to do ?

> You've spent two heart-sinking hours crammed in an overcrowded train. The bus sneered as it passed you by. You trudged like a wet shadow through the torrential rain. You arrived home soaked to the skin and looking like a sad, soggy toy koala abandoned in the street.
>
> NOW – drop your bags in the hall, kick off your shoes, leave the world of worries behind, and sink slowly into the silky-smooth, soothing waters of paradise that only Prima's Pamper Potion can provide. Add one drop. That's all it takes. So remember:
>
>   Prima washes away
>   All the cares of the day

1. Write down the **three** words in the first sentence that makes the journey home sound miserable.

   _____

2. Buses don't sneer. Why do you think the author has described the bus in that way?

   _____

3. Which word is used instead of **walked**?

   _____

4. The 2nd paragraph begins like a set of commands. Write down the imperative verbs.

   _____

5. Alliteration catches your eye when you're reading. Write down an example.

   _____

Now here is a another style of writing. The author has a different intention.

> Blood-red flares exploded from Wizard Malgor's horn-toad fingers and blazed through the swirling darkness, striking the ancient oak that had accompanied us along the lost paths of the forest known as Nabrog. Our uncommon guide crumbled to the ground with a gnarled sigh.
>
> As the moon shouldered its way through the racing clouds, we could see that Malgor had been joined by his hideous friends: the loathsome Mountain Ogres and the vile Terrawitches. All our hopes of reaching the Fountain of Life before our enemies were fading as quickly as hope reflected in the eye of a wolf.
>
> There was one chance: Seraphina Orwendyn and her army of archers. I raised the elk-horn to my lips and blew.

1. What is the effect of using strange, made-up names, such as **Malgor** and **Nabrog**?

   _____

   _____

2. The ancient oak is not like normal trees. Write down **three** words or phrases that make it seem human-like.

   _____

   _____

   _____

3. Find **two** examples of how the author has created a particular atmosphere by describing the setting.

   _____

   _____

4. **'Fading as quickly as hope reflected in the eye of a wolf.'** In this simile, whose hope is being referred to?

   _____

Again, here is another style of writing.

SHEEP
Sheep are not athletic,
They're never energetic,
But if they were magnetic,
You could stick one on the fridge.

CHICKENS
If chickens were invisible,
You'd get a huge surprise
If an egg appeared from nowhere,
Right before your eyes.

RABBIT
Rabbit looks sad in the corner of its hutch.
You never hear it complaining much.
It's too busy thinking of fields it once saw
And the escape route it's tunnelling under the straw.

NEWT
Nora Newt plays the flute -
Her Auntie Vivian says, "Clever amphibian!"

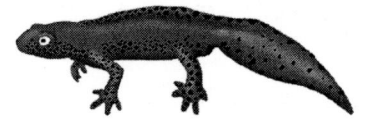

1. Which **two** poems try to entertain the reader by using unexpected rhymes?

2. In different ways, all the poems end with some sort of surprise. Choose one and describe how it surprises the reader.

3. Even without the illustrations, the writer is trying to create a picture in your head. Which poem creates the funniest picture?

4. Which poem is your favourite? Explain why.

Finally, here are some sentences that might be found in poems or different kinds of stories. Each one is followed by a question.

The wind twisted down the narrow street, whistling a lonely tune.

Are there people in the street? How do you know?

_____

Take care crossing the road, for the cars hunt like night wolves in a pack.

Which phrase is the simile, emphasising the importance of taking care?

_____

Grandma's house creaks like her knees.

Does Grandma live in an old house or a new house?

_____

Like a crow on a windowsill, the spy stood, listening.

What colour are the spy's clothes?

_____

The owls and bats pulled a curtain across the sky.

What is the 'curtain'?

_____

Our autumn walk in the woods took us across carpets of gold.

What are the 'carpets of gold'?

_____

Themes and conventions

Strand: Themes and conventions

National Curriculum reference:

- identifying themes and conventions in a wide range of books

Reading Test / Content Domain links: 2a, 2b, 2c, 2f, 2g

FIRE!

Here are some short extracts from a range of texts about fire. **Draw** lines connecting each piece of writing to the correct genre.

Last night, Sutton Fire Crew were called out to the derelict barn at Highfield Farm.	diary
I remember my first Guy Fawkes night way back in 1952. I was only four years old at the time.	myth
I don't think I'll bother speaking to Jan anymore. She said she'd bring her Dad and meet me in town to buy fireworks. It isn't the first time she's been hours late.	explanation
A sickening crack overhead. A shower of sparks. A beam burst into flames and crashed down in front of us, barring our only way out.	biography
Prometheus was the Greek god who created mankind, stealing fire from Mount Olympus and bringing it into the world of humans.	newspaper
Fire – producing light and heat – can be different colours depending on what is burning.	adventure

COMPLETE THE PICTURE

Here are a number of characters, settings and other elements that you find in different types of story. Put them into the correct frames.

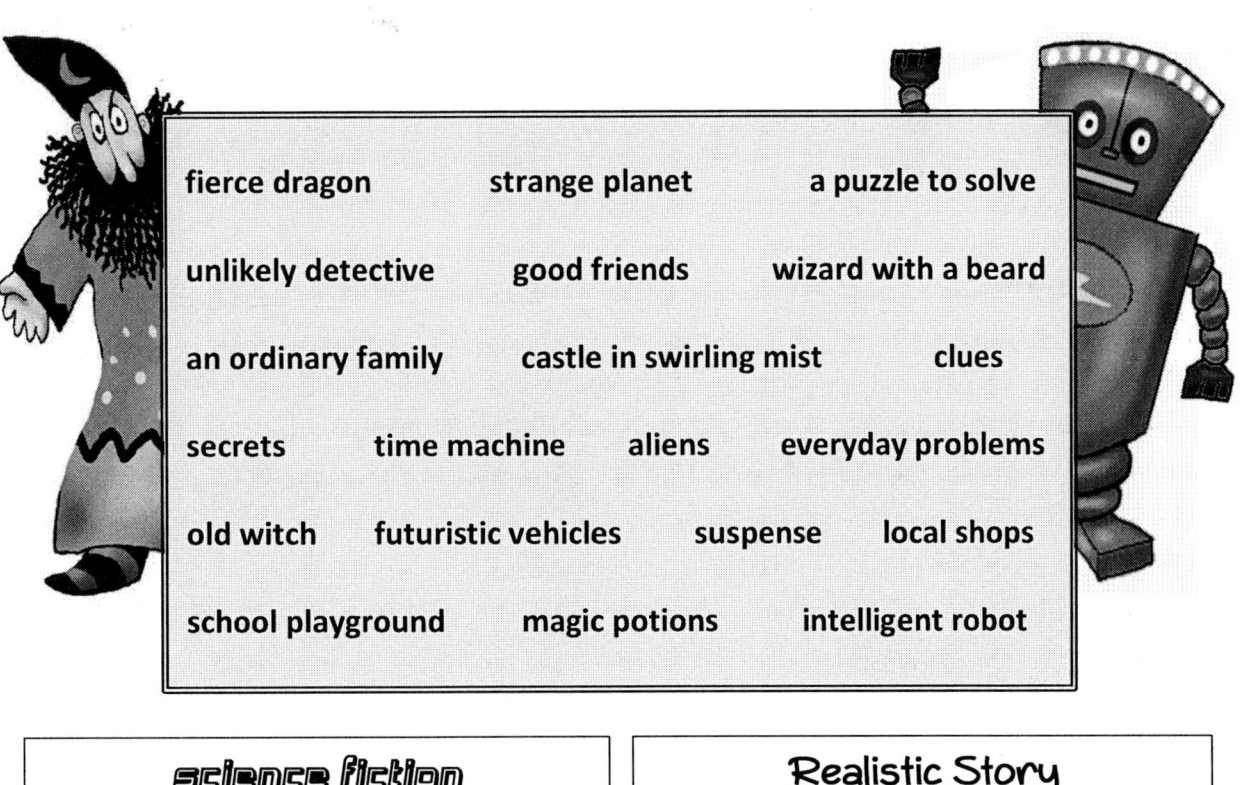

fierce dragon strange planet a puzzle to solve

unlikely detective good friends wizard with a beard

an ordinary family castle in swirling mist clues

secrets time machine aliens everyday problems

old witch futuristic vehicles suspense local shops

school playground magic potions intelligent robot

science fiction

_____
_____
_____
_____
_____

Realistic Story

_____
_____
_____
_____
_____

fantasy

_____
_____
_____
_____
_____

mystery

_____
_____
_____
_____
_____

WITNESS STATEMENTS

Here is a statement from Annie, who witnessed a strange event. Underline the elements you might expect to find in a mystery story, for example:

- a strange occurrence
- a puzzle to be solved
- clues
- false clues (called 'red herrings')
- suspects
- a final explanation   Then, at the side, label what you have found.

> I remember seeing Chuck steering a racing car just a few minutes before there was a flash and everything went dark. We had stopped at a service station on the motorway. A very helpful attendant found us a parking space. But, inside, there was nobody else there. Very odd. Oh, I don't mean it was a real racing car. No. As usual, my brother was shoving his money down the throat of some hypnotic videogame. A strange, blank look had come over him. I thought nothing of it at the time. Just a bit more zombie-like than usual.
>
> I was buying sandwiches from a shop assistant dressed as an Egyptian mummy and it wasn't even Halloween, when... what...? A power cut, I suppose. When the lights came on, Chuck had disappeared. It was only a few seconds. He didn't have time to go anywhere.
>
> When I went over to where he'd been and peered at the screen, I got such a shock. The cars were still racing round the track, but this was weird. There was Chuck. In a car. Inside the machine. Smiling his head off. Like he'd gone to digital heaven. Now, Annie, I said to myself, there has to be an explanation. Then I spotted the machine's camera option. He'd gone and photographed himself, so he could personalise the experience.
>
> But where was he? The real Chuck. Another blinding flash and the floor opened up underneath me. I slid down some kind of ramp into a room full of people, including Chuck, playing video games like mad. Young and old, all controlled by the machines. I covered my eyes in order to resist their influence. That's when I saw the car park attendant run out of another door. I quickly pulled the plug for the machines out of its socket.
>
> They all looked dazed. Even more so when they realised how much money they had fed into the machines.

Making comparisons

Strand: Make comparisons within the text

National Curriculum reference:

- making comparisons within and across books

Reading Test / Content Domain links: 2a, 2b, 2c, 2d, 2f, 2g, 2h

THE CAROL SERVICE

Here, a few different people – a pupil, a teacher, a parent and a local newspaper reporter – express their own views about how well the school carol service went.

I thought things went quite well last night. I noticed Jason arrived at the last minute, but, otherwise, I think everybody was there. Marlena as the angel was great, though I think she added a few things not in the script. We all sang well, and I've never played the recorder as well as that. Brilliant!

Three children trooped in late and two others didn't appear at all! No excuse! The children sang well enough, though they sang better during rehearsals. I've no idea what our angel was talking about on stage. I had to tell some boys off for not paying attention. They could have all looked a bit smarter too. Thank goodness the musicians played better than ever.

Weren't the children wonderful last night? A bit chatty but looked great in school uniform. One of the best Christmas services I've been to. I'm sure their teachers must be very proud of them. Marlena had a very important part. She'll surely be an actor when she grows up. The music was not bad, though I must say I'm not a big fan of the recorder.

CLASSIC CAROLS AT ST CUTHBERT'S

Local schoolchildren surpassed themselves last night at St Cuthbert's Christmas Carol Service, attended by a record number of parents and grandparents. The singing was note-perfect even if the recorders were occasionally a little flat. The whole school turned out well and the nativity play, although a few children forgot their lines, was, nonetheless, quite charming. Those pupils who had come down with a cold missed a night to remember.

Now, having compared these different points of view, how do you think each person would rate aspects of the children's performance. Put a **tick** in the appropriate box.

aspect	disappointing	good	excellent	don't know
attendance				
tidy appearance				
singing / music				
acting skills				
listening skills				

aspect	disappointing	good	excellent	don't know
attendance				
tidy appearance				
singing / music				
acting skills				
listening skills				

aspect	disappointing	good	excellent	don't know
attendance				
tidy appearance				
singing / music				
acting skills				
listening skills				

aspect	disappointing	good	excellent	don't know
attendance				
tidy appearance				
singing / music				
acting skills				
listening skills				

RAVEN REVIEWS

Read these two poems about a raven and compare their different use of words and descriptive phrases.

Raven,

in the unhappy funeral suit you stole,
you eclipsed the sun and left a black hole,
a gloomy day and a shadowy night.
Your rising wings bring darkness in flight,
like an oily rag thrown in the air.
You're a bad scallywag with a wicked stare.
Bleak, black beak tapping the tree.
You look like a dangerous gangster to me.

Black Looks

Look at me strut.
Look at me stroll.
Black as liquorice,
shiny as coal.
In this place they call
London Tower, who
comes and goes? Who has the power?
Forty-one kings and queens walked across,
but this is my patch – guess who's the boss.
So when you plan a day out with your chums,
draw me, snap me, feed me your crumbs,
remember I saw it all –
courtiers and crooks.
Say that you saw me
and the raven's
black
looks.

1. In the two poems, there are a number of ways in which the writer describes the bird's black feathers. Make a list of them.

   RAVEN   **BLACK LOOKS**

   _____   _____

   _____   _____

   _____

   _____

   _____

   _____

2. Write down a simile used in the first poem, 'Raven'.

   _____

3. The poems are told from different points of view. How are they different?

   _____

   _____

4. The second poem ends with the same words as its title – 'black looks'. Write down a similar phrase that is used in 'Raven'.

   _____

5. Find examples of phrases from both poems that suggest the raven is in charge.

   RAVEN   **BLACK LOOKS**

   _____   _____

   _____   _____

© Copyright HeadStart Primary Ltd 2016

TESTS

National Curriculum References	118
TEST A	119
The Old Toyshop	120
A History of Time	125
Some Time Underground	129
Answers and mark scheme – Test A	135
Tracking progress	138
TEST B	139
The Voyage of the Beagle	140
The Ring Of Fire	144
The Aliens are Already Here	148
Answers and mark scheme – Test B	155
Tracking progress	158
TEST C	159
Secrets of the Woods	160
The Jurassic Coast	164
A Whale of a Tale	168
Answers and mark scheme – Test C	173
Tracking progress	176

© Copyright HeadStart Primary Ltd 2016

> **Strand:** Range of texts
>
> **National Curriculum objectives:**
>
> - [listening to and] discussing a wide range of fiction, poetry, plays, non-fiction and reference books or textbooks
>
> - reading books that are structured in different ways and reading for a range of purposes
>
> - increasing their familiarity with a wide range of books, including fairy stories, myths and legends [and retelling some of these orally]
>
> **Reading Test / Content Domain links:** 2a, 2b, 2c, 2d, 2e, 2f, 2g

A note about the tests:

The KS2 English Reading Test Framework 2016 (table 9) sets out the proportion of marks for each domain, with the higher percentages given to **retrieving and recording information** and **making inferences**. This is reflected in the test questions presented here.

TEST A

YEAR 5

> The Old Toyshop
> A History of Time
> Some Time Underground

Name: _____

Class: _____

Date: _____

Raw Score [ ]   **Percentage Score** [ ] %

Teacher's Notes:

© Copyright HeadStart Primary Ltd 2016

Test A - Year 5

THE OLD TOYSHOP

Did you know that before computer games, there were plastic toys with batteries... and... before that... there were toys that you had to wind up? I've still got some in my toyshop. I know they're not as thrilling as computer games, but I like them.

Monkey

This is special. It's clockwork. Yes, you wind it up with a key and it spins two balls on plates. Also, it moves its head as if watching them. It has a metal mechanism inside, but it has a soft face made of fabric and it has a shirt, trousers and jacket as well as a hat. He's about the same age as me now. I'd never sell him. Hah! There I go again, referring to it as 'him'!

Juggling Elephant

I call this a juggling elephant, though it doesn't actually juggle. When you turn the key, the flaps at the top of its trunk spin around. At the same time, four coloured balls travel up the wire spiral on the right, slide down the little chute and fall into the round tub held by the elephant. Amazing, don't you think? Yet, if you look underneath, you can see how it works. First, you turn its key and tighten the metal spring. Then, as the spring unwinds, it turns a rod hidden inside the elephant's trunk and that makes everything move.

Clown

This clown is just one example of comical characters you might come across riding a three-wheeled bike. The clever thing about it, however, is that it doesn't just scoot off in one direction. It stops and starts and changes direction when you least expect it. Little kids always want to take one home.

Russian Princess

What you can't see in this photograph are the tiny wheels on the bottom of the princess's tin-plate dress. This enables her to spin around like a dancer, as if she had a mind of her own. She is often decorated in what looks like traditional Russian clothes. A collector on the look-out for this sort of toy would find them painted in different colours and patterns.

I don't know what to call this car made by a boy from a poor area in South Africa. He collected old food cans, flattened them and cut them into shapes to fit together. It doesn't move on its own, but the boot and bonnet open up. Brilliant!

© Copyright HeadStart Primary Ltd 2016

Test A - Year 5

1. Look at the introduction in the form of Tim's speech bubble. What is the main point he is making? **Tick one** box.

   He owns a toyshop. ☐

   Computer games are thrilling. ☐

   There are different types of toys. ☐

   1 mark

2. Which toy do you think is Tim's favourite?

   _____

   1 mark

3. What does the Monkey do when you wind it up?
   Tick two.

   It smiles. ☐

   It spins balls on plates. ☐

   Its body twists and turns. ☐

   It moves its head. ☐

   2 marks

4. Tim talks about two of his toys as if they were people.
   Which **two**?

   1) _____

   2) _____

   2 marks

Test A - Year 5

5. In his description of the Juggling Elephant, Tim explains how it works. Number the different steps in the correct order.

☐ the spring unwinds

☐ everything moves

☐ you turn its key

1 mark

6. In the description of the Juggling Elephant, the word **rotates** is used. **Circle** a word that has a similar meaning.

bends   turns   tightens

1 mark

7. Tim mentions **two** sorts of customers who would be interested in his toys. Who are they?

1) _____

2) _____

2 marks

8. Look at the information about the Russian Princess. Write down **two ways** in which Russian Princess toys might be painted differently.

1) _____

2) _____

2 marks

Test A - Year 5

9. More than once, Tim hints at how much he likes these toys. Write down **two** things he says that show you how he feels.

   1) _____

   2) _____

   2 marks

10. Which **two** toys move in unexpected directions?

    1) _____

    2) _____

    1 mark

11. Tim and the Monkey both have a hat. Tim says there is something else that they have in common. What is it?

    _____

    1 mark

12. Tim says **two** parts of the car move. What are they?

    1) _____

    2) _____

    1 mark

13. Why do you think the South African boy made his car from flattened food cans?

    _____

    _____

    2 marks

© Copyright HeadStart Primary Ltd 2016

14. Help Tim out by thinking of a good title for the car.

_____   _____
                                                     1 mark

...... A HISTORY OF TIME ......

Test A - Year 5

Before time was measured in seconds, minutes and hours, people relied on the sun, the moon and the seasons. Work started at sunrise and finished at sunset. Changes in the seasons told farmers when to plant and when to harvest. As there were no clocks, it would have made no sense to say: "I'll meet you at two o'clock."

People watched how the sun seemed to move across the sky. They realised that smaller amounts of time could be measured by the changing position of the shadow of a stick pushed into the ground: the sundial! This led to more accurate versions. An Egyptian sundial from 800 BC still exists, but they were known and used by astronomers even before this date.

The trouble with sundials is that they are no use at night or when the sun isn't shining. Also, at different times of the year, the sun is higher or lower in the sky, affecting the shadow formed by the sundial. The Greeks and others tried to solve this problem. They invented the *clepsydra* or water clock. The problem with this, however, was that trying to regulate the drips of water that fell into a tank, which then turned the clock pointer, was impossible.

Their popularity with some scientists and wealthy people continued, but they saw them as toys rather than something that told the time.

The hourglass works in a similar way to the water clock, using sand instead of water. People often used them to time the length of sermons from the church pulpit. They are still used today as egg-timers and in board games. They have the advantage of being able to be used at night by the light of the moon or a candle.

The creation of an accurate mechanical clock was the dream of astronomers and inventors in the 13th and 14th centuries. The clock in Salisbury Cathedral, installed around 1386, is still working. Having no clock face, it operates a bell that strikes the hours. (The word *clock* is similar to the French word *cloche*, meaning *bell*.)

The invention of mechanical clocks not only led to the clocks that we are familiar with today, but also to our idea of time, itself. With the more recent addition of digital clocks and watches, as well as other displays on mobiles, computers, car dashboards and in public places, we are more aware than ever of time passing, time lost, time wasted and no time to do everything that we would like. Are we like the White Rabbit in *Alice in Wonderland* – always in a hurry?

Test A - Year 5

1. Before clocks, how would people have worked out the length of a working day?

   _____

   1 mark

2. 'People watched how the sun **seemed** to move across the sky.' Why has the writer used the word **seemed**?

   _____

   _____

   1 mark

3. Describe how a simple version of a sundial works.

   _____

   _____

   1 mark

4. What are the **two** main problems with sundials?

   1) _____

   2) _____

   _____

   2 marks

5. What is another name for a **clepsydra**?

   _____

   1 mark

© Copyright HeadStart Primary Ltd 2016

Test A - Year 5

6. The problem with water clocks was 'trying to **regulate** the drips of water that fell into the tank'. **Circle** a word that is similar in meaning to **regulate**.

    stop   control   design

1 mark

7. Water clocks were not good at telling the time. The text suggests the type of person who continued to enjoy them. Write down **one** type of person.

_____

1 mark

8. Give an example from the text of how hourglasses are used today.

_____

1 mark

9. In what way is an hourglass better than a water clock?

_____

_____

1 mark

10. One of the earliest mechanical clocks was installed in Salisbury Cathedral. How is it different from clocks today?

_____

_____

1 mark

© Copyright HeadStart Primary Ltd 2016

11. Look at the last paragraph. What is it mainly about?
    Tick one box.

    Mechanical clocks have been replaced by digital clocks. ☐

    Clocks make us more aware of time passing. ☐

    There is no time to do everything. ☐

    1 mark

12. Read the last sentence again. How is it different from the rest of this historical account? **Tick one** box.

    The writer is expressing a personal view. ☐

    The writer is recommending *Alice in Wonderland*. ☐

    The writer is ending with a joke. ☐

    1 mark

Some Time Underground
part 1

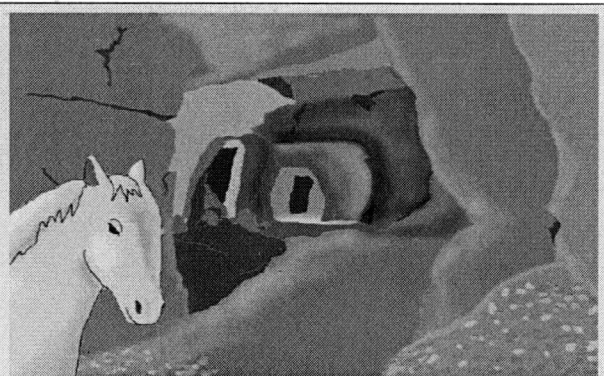

"I don't want to waste any time telling you to stop chatting and listen," says the guide. Not that anybody, apart from Luke, that is, is chatting. His voice is bouncing round the cavernous stone mine like a mad bunny. They call them quarries here in Bath, but they're like underground mines and just a tad spooky, if you ask me.

"He's looking at me, Joanie. I never said a word."

"Yeah, right." There's something about my own echo – the words circling round and coming back that makes my head buzz. Or maybe it's the thought of being underground and standing next to a water barrel for the horses that used to haul out the blocks of limestone. Heavy blocks that were shaped and cut to build all the houses here, ever since Roman times. All of those houses above the earth that left miles and miles of corridors and caverns under the earth. It's making my brain go funny.

"Of course, where you're all standing was once an ocean. Perhaps your teacher has already explained that limestone is the result of dead sea creatures sinking to the bottom of the ocean, layer upon layer." The voice of the guide sounds far away.

The water barrel is encrusted with its own stalactites and stalagmites. Years of rainwater seeping through the limestone roof of this man-made cave. I have to put my hands on it.

"Joanie?" says Luke. I can see his outline, but his face is in shadow. "You all right?"

"These mine workings," says the guide, "have been stable for a hundred and fifty years, but, in case of emergencies, I'll blow this whistle and you will all walk, I said *walk*, behind me to a safe place. And another thing..."

I can hear some of what he is saying, but there is a tingling in my fingers, spreading up my arms to my neck. He's talking about how these spaces beneath the earth were used for storage, and, especially, for ammunition during the war. And there's something else.

"A ghost, Joanie. Did you hear what he said about an old miner and his horse?"

There is a sudden and ear-shattering rumble of falling rock, or as if a train were racing towards us – straight towards us – down one of the many tunnels. There is panic! The whistle! Elbows, scuffling feet, screams, the whistle, rumbling. I'm pushed to the floor. Then silence. No train, no rock fall and no one. I'm alone. Completely alone.

part 2

I have my torch, but which path do I take? "Luke!" His name comes firing back from all directions, like a chorus of jeering kids. I can hear something else: sounds of work going on, like crates being shifted, men talking. I pick my way over chunks of stone, guessing at corners, while all the time terrible shadows leap around the walls.

The voices are getting closer and there is more light. Up ahead, men are working to unload a train. A freight train has stopped inside a railway tunnel, beside an entrance to this stone mine. Crates are being manhandled from an open carriage onto an old jeep.

"Jenkins!" The shriek, so close to my ear, makes me jump. "Jenkins, stop slacking and get over there. That train's got to be on its way before the enemy gets suspicious." The man is wearing some sort of uniform. He has some stripes on his sleeve. More than that, I can't say, because, somehow, a sense of urgency has taken me over. I don't know who Jenkins is, but those crates have to be unloaded as soon as possible. The contents are priceless. They must not get into the wrong hands. I know that much. Somehow.

We work as fast as we can – these soldiers and me. As two of us lift off the final crate, I stare down at the royal seal on the lid. Something precious inside. I let my side slip, ripping off one of the metal buttons from the jacket of the soldier helping me. He smiles and shakes his head. Then I bend down to pick it up, but he is no longer there. The jeep has vanished. There is no train. No opening to a railway tunnel.

I wander, maybe for an hour, desperately lost. Somebody must come looking for me. The batteries in my torch are fading and so are my hopes.

One of the shadows is moving. A human shape. I think my heart will leave my body. For the shape speaks. "You lost, dear?" I think my mouth is open. I can't tell. I can't hear anything coming out. "Don't worry. It happens. Charlie, here, he's old and can't see very well, but he'll take you back."

Charlie is white and seems to shimmer. I hold onto his mane and off we trundle through pitch black corridors until we reach the water barrel. I'm so thankful to recognise something, I want to feel it to make sure it is real. A voice whispers in my ear, "You'll be fine now." When I turn, there's Luke and the others. A glimmer of light and Charlie melts into the darker corners.

"Now," says the guide, "remember I was saying that the government and the army stored a lot of top-secret stuff down here. Well, there was something kept here during the Second World War... you'll never guess..."

I lean over to Luke. "Crown jewels," I say.

Luke laughs and gets a hard stare from the guide. "Don't be so stu..." he whispers.

"Crown jewels," interrupts the guide. "Only a few people at the time knew about it. The perfect hiding place. Box Tunnel is a few miles in that direction. The train would enter, stop, then unload, before trundling out at the other end. Top secret."

There's a puzzled expression on Luke's face. I smile as my fingers trace the outline of the metal button in my pocket.

Test A - Year 5

1. Who are being shown by the guide round the underground limestone quarries?

   _____

   1 mark

2. When Luke says, 'I never said a word', why does Joanie say, 'Yeah, right'?

   _____

   _____

   1 mark

3. How have these underground caverns been created?
   Tick one:

   natural caves where people have lived ☐

   holes in the rock eroded by the sea ☐

   rock has been removed to build houses ☐

   1 mark

4. In the 3rd paragraph, beginning **'Yeah, right'**, there are **two** phrases describing how Joanie feels that suggest some strange adventure is about to happen to her. What are those phrases?

   1) _____

   2) _____

   2 marks

© Copyright HeadStart Primary Ltd 2016

Test A - Year 5

5. The guide talks about limestone. Describe how it is formed.

   _____

   _____

   1 mark

6. When Joanie puts her hands on the water barrel, she hears only some of what the guide is saying. What sensations does she feel in different parts of her body?

   1) _____

   2) _____

   2 marks

7. In the last paragraph of **Part 1**, write down an example of a simile being used to create a sense of danger.

   _____

   1 mark

8. At the beginning of **Part 2**, Joanie says she can hear different sounds. **Tick** the sound that she **does not hear**.

   crates being shifted ☐

   rock falling ☐

   men talking ☐

   1 mark

9. Who do you think shouts 'Jenkins!' at Joanie?

   _____

   1 mark

© Copyright HeadStart Primary Ltd 2016

10. Write down **one** of the clues you used to answer **question 9**.

_____

_____

1 mark

11. The writer doesn't say who the **two** are who help Joanie when she is lost. Who do you think they are?

1) _____

2) _____

2 marks

12. At the end of the story, Luke is puzzled as Joanie smiles and touches the metal button in her pocket.
We don't know what she is thinking.
What could she be thinking?

_____

_____

_____

3 marks

Answers and Mark Scheme – Test A – Year 5

The Old Toyshop			
No.	Answers and Mark Scheme	Domain	Marks
1	There are different types of toys.	2c	1
2	Monkey	2d	1
3	1. It spins balls on plates. = 1 mark 2. It moves its head. = 1 mark	2b	2
4	Monkey = 1 mark Russian Princess = 1 mark	2b	2
5	1. you turn its key 2. the spring unwinds 3. everything moves	2c	1
6	turns	2a	1
7	little kids = 1 mark collectors = 1 mark	2b	2
8	colours = 1 mark patterns = 1 mark	2b	2
9	I'd never sell him. (Monkey) Amazing, don't you think? (Elephant) Brilliant! (Car) [Award 2 marks for any two correct answers; 1 mark for one correct answer.]	2d	2
10	Clown and Russian Princess	2b	1
11	They are the same age.	2b	1
12	boot and bonnet	2b	1
13	He was too poor to buy a toy car from a shop, [= 1 mark] and so he made his own from materials freely available / by recycling cans. [= 1 mark]	2d	2
14	Any title that encapsulates features and materials of the toy, how it was made, or who made it, or Tim's word: 'brilliant'.	2c	1

© Copyright HeadStart Primary Ltd 2016

A History of Time			
No.	Answers and Mark Scheme	Domain	Marks
1	They would use the sun, the moon and the seasons. / It started at sunrise and finished at sunset.	2b	1
2	Despite appearances, the Earth orbits the sun.	2d	1
3	You can observe the changing position of the shadow of a stick in the ground.	2b	1
4	They are no use when the sun isn't shining. = 1 mark At different times of the year, the shadow will be affected by how high or how low the sun is in the sky. = 1 mark	2b	2
5	water clock	2b	1
6	control	2a	1
7	some scientists / wealthy people	2b	1
8	board games / egg-timers	2b	1
9	It can be used at night.	2b	1
10	It has no clock face.	2b	1
11	Clocks make us more aware of time passing.	2c	1
12	The writer is expressing a personal view.	2f	1

Some Time Underground			
No.	Answers and Mark Scheme	Domain	Marks
1	Joanie and Luke / sister and brother / a group of children on a school trip	2b / 2d	1
2	She doesn't believe him. / He was talking.	2d	1
3	rock has been removed to build houses	2b	1
4	makes my head buzz = 1 mark It's making my brain go funny. = 1 mark	2g	2
5	Limestone is the result of dead creatures sinking to the bottom of the sea.	2b	1
6	there is a tingling in my fingers, [= 1 mark] spreading up my arms to my neck [= 1 mark]	2g	2
7	as if a train were racing towards us	2g	1
8	rock falling	2b	1
9	army officer / wartime official / sergeant / soldier	2d	1
10	The man is wearing some sort of uniform. / He has some stripes on his sleeve.	2d	1
11	The ghost of an old quarryman / miner. = 1 mark The old quarryman's ghostly horse / Charlie. = 1 mark	2d	2
12	It is evidence / a real object [= 1 mark] from a soldier's uniform / linked to the past and the wartime use of the underground quarries. [= 1 mark] Joanie believes her experience was real. / This is how she knew the crown jewels were involved. [= 1 mark]	2d	3
		TOTAL	50

Tracking – using tests to track children's progress

Once a test has been marked, a score out of 50 can be awarded. This score should then be converted to a percentage.

The table below can then be used to identify progress against one of the 6 stages. The table uses percentage scores for conversion.

Year 5

Percentage Score	Stage	
0 – 25	Emerging	Less than expected progress
26 – 50	Developing	
51 – 63	Progressing	Expected progress
64 – 75	Secure	
76 – 88	Mastering	More than expected progress
89 – 100	Exceeding	

```
0 – 50%        Less than expected
51 – 75%       Expected
76 – 100%      More than expected
```

The assessments are intended to be used by teachers as a tool to support their professional judgement. The table above should be used only as a guide to achievement and progress. This data should always be used in conjunction with ongoing teacher assessment.

TEST B

YEAR 5

The Voyage of the Beagle
The Ring of Fire
The Aliens are Already Here!

Name: _____

Class: _____

Date: _____

Raw Score [ ]   **Percentage Score** [ ] %

Teacher's Notes:

Test B - Year 5

The Voyage of the Beagle

The portrait of Charles Darwin on the left shows him as a young man of around 27 years old. In 1836, he had just returned from a voyage on board the Beagle, captained by Robert FitzRoy. During the five-year trip to South America, Captain FitzRoy made maps of the coastline. Darwin, on the other hand, was interested in collecting specimens to learn more about animals.

The portrait on the right shows Darwin when he was 60 years old. By then, he had written *On the Origin of the Species* – a book that changed the way people thought about life on Earth.

During the voyage, Syms Covington, the ship's fiddler and cabin boy, noted the following:

> On the morning of 27th December, 1831, H.M.S. Beagle, with a crew of seventy-three men, sailed out of Plymouth harbour under a calm easterly wind and drizzly rain. Darwin became seasick almost immediately and started to have second thoughts about the voyage.

Syms Covington, however, was of great help to Darwin, especially when they landed on the volcanic islands of the Galapagos. Covington helped him by keeping notes of the different species and where they were found.

Darwin realised that many of the creatures and plants found on the islands were the same as those on the South American mainland, but they had changed. They had changed over time (evolved) to suit conditions on the islands. The beaks of songbirds, for instance, had adapted to the type of food they ate.

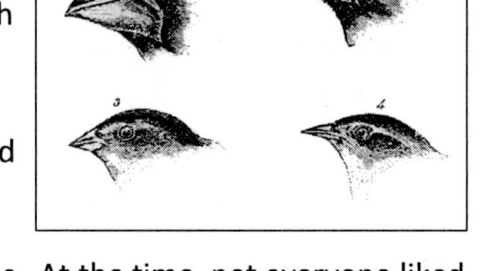

He later argued that human beings had evolved from apes. At the time, not everyone liked this new idea. Nonetheless, the survival of any species of animal or plant depends on how well it adapts to its environment. Watch any nature programme today to see how true this is.

© Copyright HeadStart Primary Ltd 2016

Test B - Year 5

1. How old is Darwin in the portrait on the left?

   _____

   1 mark

2. What was the name of the captain of the Beagle?

   _____

   1 mark

3. What was the captain's reason for sailing to South America? **Tick one.**

   to map the coastline ☐

   to collect specimens ☐

   to observe animals ☐

   1 mark

4. Darwin's book, *On the Origin of the Species,* changed the way people thought about things. What changed?

   _____

   _____

   1 mark

5. Darwin was not an experienced sailor. Write down **two** clues.

   1) _____

   2) _____

   2 marks

© Copyright HeadStart Primary Ltd 2016

6. Who was Syms Covington?

 _____

 1 mark

7. How did Covington help Darwin during the voyage?

 _____

 _____

 1 mark

8. What word is used to describe the Galapagos islands?

 _____

 1 mark

9. What does **evolve** mean? **Tick one.**

 turn around ☐

 change over time ☐

 involve ☐

 1 mark

10. The writer has included an illustration from Darwin's book showing the beaks of songbirds.
 Why do you think this has been included?

 _____

 _____

 2 marks

11. Later, Darwin came up with a new idea that not everyone liked. What was it?

_____

_____

1 mark

Test B - Year 5

THE RING OF FIRE

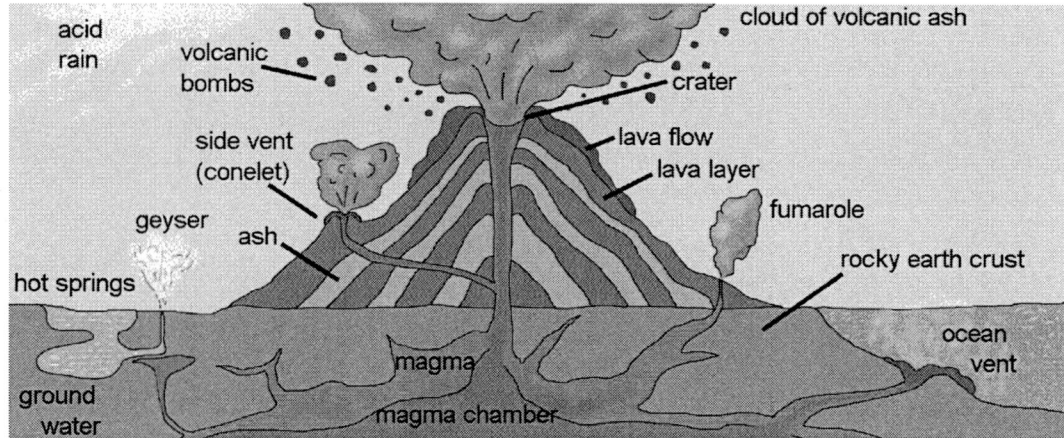

WHAT IS A VOLCANO?
A volcano is created when magma from deep inside the Earth works its way up to the surface, erupting into a cloud of gas, ash and lava. Noxious gases result in acid rain. The lava and ash add layers around a cone or smaller side vents. With each eruption, the volcano grows in size.

WHY DO VOLCANOES ERUPT?
The surface of the Earth is made up of enormous plates that slide incredibly slowly over molten rock. These are called *tectonic plates*. These plates move in different directions. This means they rub against each other and sometimes collide. This leads to earthquakes and volcanic activity.

PAST ERUPTIONS
The loudest sound in modern history was caused by Krakatoa in Indonesia in 1883. After several small eruptions, the main explosion took place on 26th and 27th of August and was heard 3000 miles away. These eruptions led to 30m high tsunamis along the coasts of Java and Sumatra, killing 32,000 people. 165 villages were destroyed. It's possible that 120,000 people were killed altogether. Volcanic gases reached high up in the atmosphere, altering weather around the world for five years.
In 1927, a new volcano was born in the same place – Anak Krakatau (Child of Krakatoa) – the unpredictable child of a very bad-tempered parent!

WHAT IS THE RING OF FIRE?
The Ring of Fire is the name given to the horseshoe shape that is formed by the countries that lie west, north and east of the Pacific Ocean. It is here that the action of different tectonic plates has produced 90% of the world's earthquakes.
It is also the site of 75% of the world's volcanoes that are either active or dormant (inactive but still liable to erupt in the future).
Volcanic islands include Hawaii and the Galapagos. In Hawaii, Mauna Kea, the world's biggest volcano, is considered to be dormant. Here, in the UK, Edinburgh Castle sits on a volcanic core – long extinct.

© Copyright HeadStart Primary Ltd 2016

Test B - Year 5

1. Finish this sentence:
   During an eruption, volcanic clouds are full of...

   _____ ,

   _____ ,

   and _____ .

   2 marks

2. **Circle** a word that means the same as **noxious**.

   explosive   poisonous   nocturnal

   1 mark

3. Look at **WHY DO VOLCANOES ERUPT?**
   Explain how the movements of tectonic plates lead to volcanic activity.

   _____

   _____

   _____

   2 marks

4. 'The loudest sound in modern history was caused by Krakatoa...'
   How far away was the explosion heard?

   _____

   1 mark

© Copyright HeadStart Primary Ltd 2016

Test B - Year 5

5. This page is from a non-fiction book.
Tick the features that tell you this is non-fiction.

diagram with labels ☐

conversations ☐

numbers and percentages ☐

explanations ☐

interesting characters ☐

2 marks

6. Describe **two** of the terrible results of Krakatoa erupting.

1) _____

2) _____

2 marks

7. Number these events in the order in which they happened in Indonesia in 1883.

☐ small eruptions

☐ tsunami

☐ main explosion

1 mark

8. As well as volcanoes, what other destructive thing happens in The Ring of Fire?

_____

1 mark

© Copyright HeadStart Primary Ltd 2016

Test B - Year 5

9. Name two sets of islands inside the Ring of Fire.

   1) _____

   2) _____

   1 mark

10. Draw lines to show whether these volcanic sites are active, dormant or extinct.

    | Anak Krakatau | | extinct |
    | Edinburgh Castle Rock | | dormant |
    | Mauna Kea | | active |

    1 mark

11. In **PAST ERUPTIONS**, what is described as **a very bad-tempered parent?**

    _____

    1 mark

© Copyright HeadStart Primary Ltd 2016

The Aliens Are Already Here!

Test B - Year 5

Some children in Class 5 have discovered that there are strange-looking creatures living right here on our planet. Each child has done a poster. Together they add up to a database of quite alien forms of life on Earth. There are eight altogether. Answer the questions about the posters on this page before you tackle the ones that follow.

Leaf-tailed Gecko

Location: Madagascar.
Dimensions: 7 – 15cm.
Habitat: in tropical forests – its green / brown colour provides camouflage among leaves.
Diet: a nocturnal reptile, with adhesive scales under its toes and large eyes, it quickly finds insects such as crickets and moths at night.
Predators: owls, rats and snakes – although the gecko can re-grow its tail if necessary; also badly affected by mass deforestation.
Feature: no eyelids; cleans eyes with tongue.

Flying Snake

Location: South-East Asia.
Dimensions: 5 different species – smallest is 60cm; largest is 1.2m.
Habitat: mainly in trees. It launches itself into the air, flattening its body and slithering to control its landing as much as 100m away.
Diet: mildly venomous, they prey on lizards, frogs, birds and bats. (Harmless to humans.)
Predators: King cobras and kraits (a highly poisonous snake).

Star-nosed Mole

Location: North America.
Dimensions: 15 – 20cm.
Habitat: in tunnels up to 270m long in moist soil, wet meadows, marshes, forest clearings.
Diet: it detects worms, slugs and small insects using the 22 sensitive tentacles of its nose. In streams and lakes, it finds amphibians and small fish. It will swim under ice in winter.
Predators: owls, hawks, skunks and weasels catch them on land (as well as dogs and cats); in water, they are preyed upon by mink.

Leafy Sea Dragon

Location: off the south coast of Australia.
Dimensions: up to 35cm with leaf-shaped frills all over their body, blending in with seaweed.
Habitat: among kelp-covered rocks.
Diet: its nose is a long pipe through which it sucks in tiny shrimps and plankton.
Predators: mainly human divers, taking them as souvenirs to such an extent that they are now a protected species.
Feature: after breeding the male, like sea horses, carries the eggs under its tail.

© Copyright HeadStart Primary Ltd 2016

Test B - Year 5

1. Which **two** creatures blend in well with their surroundings?

   1) _____

   2) _____

   1 mark

2. What word describes the Leaf-tailed Gecko's habit of hunting at night?

   _____

   1 mark

3. How does the Flying Snake fly and land safely?

   _____

   _____

   2 marks

4. Which **two** creatures are hunted by snakes?

   1) _____

   2) _____

   2 marks

5. What does **deforestation** mean?

   _____

   1 mark

6. Which **two** animals are at risk from human beings and their pets?

   1) _____

   2) _____

   2 marks

© Copyright HeadStart Primary Ltd 2016

7. The noses of the Star-nosed Mole and the Leafy Sea Dragon are very important. Describe how each creature uses them.

Star-nosed Mole	Leafy Sea Dragon

2 marks

Here are the posters of four more strange creatures. Read about them, then answer the questions that follow on the next page.

Test B - Year 5

Axolotl

Location: in lakes near Mexico City.
Dimensions: 15-45cm, though over 30cm is rare.
Habitat: under rocks and in crevices at the bottom of lakes, with the result that they are often white or pink.
Diet: its diet includes small crabs, molluscs, worms and small fish.
Predators: because they remain at the bottom of lakes, they have few predators, though storks and herons will take them if they can. Fish, such as carp will eat their young. Human beings also take them as pets.
Features: often known as the Mexican Walking Fish, they are amphibians. Like newts, they are able to regrow damaged limbs.

Blue Dragon

Location: wherever winds and currents take it.
Dimensions: up to 3cm.
Habitat: on the surface of the sea, floating upside-down.
Diet: the venomous Portuguese Man of War and other jellyfish.
Predators: potential predators of this sea slug can receive a concentration of jellyfish poison it stores in its skin.
Features: a special gas-filled sac in its stomach enables it to float.

Streaked Tenrec

Location: Madagascar.
Dimensions: 16-19cm.
Habitat: in burrows 1.5m long near a stream or lake. It covers the entrance with leaves.
Diet: foraging for food mainly at night, it eats insects and worms.
Predators: mainly the mongoose, although the tenrec has detachable spines which it uses to drive into its attacker's nose or paws.
Features: It communicates by squeaking, stamping its feet, and rubbing together special spines to produce a high-pitched sound heard by other tenrecs.

Japanese Spider Crab

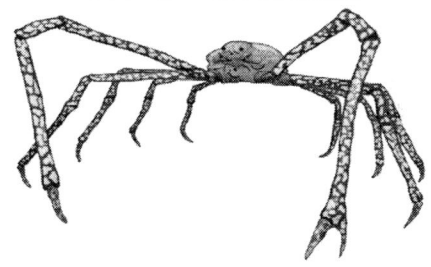

Location: the seas around Japan.
Dimensions: the leg span of this giant crab can reach 3.8m.
Habitat: 300m deep on the rocky and sandy bottom of the sea close to the islands.
Diet: despite its fiercesome size, it eats small shellfish and the remains of dead animals.
Predators: their size deters most predators. When they are caught up in fishing nets, they can end up as spider crab sushi in restaurants.
Features: not only does the crab's bumpy armour-plating blend in with the rocks, it also adorns itself with sponges and seaweed to boost its camouflage.

© Copyright HeadStart Primary Ltd 2016

Test B - Year 5

1. Which one of these four animals is the smallest and the most dangerous?

   _____

   1 mark

2. Which animals prey on the axolotl?

   _____

   1 mark

3. Which **two** animals have most to fear from human beings?

   1) _____

   2) _____

   1 mark

4. Describe the **three** different ways in which the Streaked Tenrec communicates.

   1) _____

   2) _____

   3) _____

   3 marks

5. Describe how the Blue Dragon protects itself.

   _____

   _____

   2 marks

6. How does the Blue Dragon keep itself afloat?

   _____

   1 mark

© Copyright HeadStart Primary Ltd 2016

7. Describe **two ways** in which the Japanese Spider Crab blends in with its surroundings.

1) _____

_____

2) _____

_____

2 marks

Answers and Mark Scheme – Test B – Year 5

The Voyage of the Beagle

No.	Answers and Mark Scheme	Domain	Marks
1	(around) 27 years old	2b	1
2	FitzRoy	2b	1
3	to map the coastline	2b	1
4	It changed the way people thought about life on Earth.	2b	1
5	(Covington points out that) Darwin became seasick [= 1 mark] and had second thoughts about the voyage. [= 1 mark]	2d	2
6	ship's fiddler and cabin boy	2b	1
7	He kept notes of the different species and where they were found.	2b	1
8	volcanic	2b	1
9	change over time	2a	1
10	(It's a diagram) showing examples of different birds' beaks, [= 1 mark] providing evidence / illustrating Darwin's discoveries / of the way animals adapt to their environment / surroundings. [= 1 mark]	2f	2
11	He argued that human beings had evolved from apes.	2b	1

© Copyright HeadStart Primary Ltd 2016

The Ring of Fire			
No.	Answers and Mark Scheme	Domain	Marks
1	gas, ash and lava [Award 2 marks for three correct answers; 1 mark for any two correct answers.]	2b	2
2	poisonous	2a	1
3	Plates rub against each other [= 1 mark] and sometimes collide. [= 1 mark]	2b	2
4	3000 miles away	2b	1
5	diagram with labels, numbers and percentages, explanations [Award 2 marks for three correct answers; 1 mark for any two correct answers. Deduct 1 mark for each incorrect answer.]	2f	2
6	30m high tsunamis (killing 32,000 people) / 165 villages were destroyed / 120,000 people killed altogether / weather altered around the world for 5 years [Award 2 marks for any two correct answers; 1 mark for one correct answer.]	2b	2
7	1. small eruptions 2. main explosion 3. tsunami	2c	1
8	earthquakes	2b	1
9	Hawaii and the Galapagos.	2b	1
10	Anak Krakatau — active Edinburgh Castle Rock — extinct Mauna Kea — dormant	2h	1
11	Krakatoa	2d	1

\multicolumn{4}{l	}{The Aliens Are Already Here!}
No.	Answers and Mark Scheme	Domain	Marks
1	Leaf-tailed Gecko and Leafy Sea Dragon	2b	1
2	nocturnal	2a	1
3	It launches itself into the air, flattens its body [= 1 mark] and slithers to control its landing. [= 1 mark]	2b	2
4	Leaf-tailed Gecko = 1 mark Flying Snake = 1 mark	2h	2
5	Cutting down / removing trees / destroying forest habitat.	2a	1
6	Leafy Sea Dragon = 1 mark Star-nosed Mole = 1 mark	2b	2
7	The Mole detects food / prey using sensitive tentacles on its nose. = 1 mark The Dragon uses its nose to suck up tiny shrimps and plankton. = 1 mark	2h	2
1	Blue Dragon	2b	1
2	storks, herons, carp	2b	1
3	Axolotl and Japanese Spider Crab	2b	1
4	squeaking = 1 mark stamping feet = 1 mark rubbing together special spines to produce a high-pitched sound = 1 mark	2b	3
5	Predators can receive a concentration of jellyfish poison [= 1 mark] that it stores in its skin. [= 1 mark]	2b	2
6	It has a special gas-filled sac in its stomach.	2b	1
7	It has bumpy armour-plating. = 1 mark It adorns itself with sponges and seaweed. = 1 mark	2b	2
		TOTAL	50

© Copyright HeadStart Primary Ltd 2016

Tracking – using tests to track children's progress

Once a test has been marked, a score out of 50 can be awarded. This score should then be converted to a percentage.

The table below can then be used to identify progress against one of the 6 stages. The table uses percentage scores for conversion.

Year 5

Percentage Score	Stage	
0 – 25	Emerging	Less than expected progress
26 – 50	Developing	
51 – 63	Progressing	Expected progress
64 – 75	Secure	
76 – 88	Mastering	More than expected progress
89 – 100	Exceeding	

```
0 – 50%        Less than expected
51 – 75%       Expected
76 – 100%      More than expected
```

The assessments are intended to be used by teachers as a tool to support their professional judgement. The table above should be used only as a guide to achievement and progress. This data should always be used in conjunction with ongoing teacher assessment.

TEST C

YEAR 5

Secrets of the Woods
The Jurassic Coast
A Whale of a Tale

Name: _____

Class: _____

Date: _____

Raw Score [ ]   **Percentage Score** [ ] %

Teacher's Notes:

SECRETS OF THE WOODS

Test C - Year 5

INTRODUCTION

Think of woodlands as magical places – a world of mystery, waiting to be discovered. Make the most of your walk in the woods. Explore its secrets. Find out how every part of it, from tiny life-forms in the soil to the leafy canopy at the top of the trees, contributes to life in the woods.

CANOPY

Trees try to maximise the amount of light reaching them. So they form a canopy of leaves at the top of their branches. The branches of trees next to each other overlap, providing safe routes through the woods for birds and animals such as squirrels. Spreading leaves also limit the amount of light that reaches plants on the ground.

TREE TRUNKS

Cracks and crevices in bark provide homes for lots of insects and food for birds, such as woodpeckers, tree creepers and nuthatches. Bigger holes offer protection for roosting bats and the nests of owls and others.

UNDERSTOREY

At a lower level are bushes that have adapted to grow in darker conditions by sprawling sideways to increase their chances of receiving light. They often provide berries and nuts for animals. Other climbing plants – honeysuckle and ivy – use existing bushes and trees to climb up towards the light.

DEAD WOOD

Fallen, rotting branches provide a home for mosses, lichens and fungi (that need little light), and a wide range of insects and other invertebrates.

FLOWERS AND HERBS

If enough light reaches the woodland floor, you will find bluebells, primroses and ferns.

SOIL

Soil provides water, nutrients and anchorage for roots. It is also the habitat of a large amount of microscopic life.

LEAF LITTER

This layer protects the soil from erosion and is a source of food and nesting materials.

© Copyright HeadStart Primary Ltd 2016

Test C - Year 5

1. In woodland, where is the **leafy canopy**?

   _____

   1 mark

2. Write down **two** phrases from the **INTRODUCTION** that are there to persuade the reader to go for a walk in the woods.

   1) _____

   2) _____

   2 marks

3. Look at **CANOPY**. It describes how the branches of trees overlap. How does this help squirrels?

   _____

   _____

   1 mark

4. What advantage do tall trees have over smaller plants?

   _____

   1 mark

5. How have bushes adapted to cope with lower amounts of light?

   _____

   1 mark

© Copyright HeadStart Primary Ltd 2016

Test C - Year 5

6. Woodlands provide lots of food for animals. Describe **two** of the foods mentioned in the text and where in the woods they are found.

food	where it is found in the woods

2 marks

7. Flowers such as bluebells and primroses are found in woods. According to the text, what must they have in order to grow?

_____

1 mark

8. Write down **two** things nesting birds find useful in woodland.

1) _____

2) _____

2 marks

9. Write down **two** things you are likely to find among rotting branches.

1) _____

2) _____

1 mark

© Copyright HeadStart Primary Ltd 2016

10. The word **anchorage** in the section on **SOIL** comes from the word **anchor**. How is it used here? **Tick one.**

the trees are prevented from moving in the wind ☐

the trees draw up water through their roots ☐

the roots stop the tree from blowing over ☐

1 mark

11. What is special about the way ivy grows?

_____

_____

1 mark

12. How does leaf litter protect the soil?

_____

1 mark

13. Most of the boxes of information have arrows attached to them. Why do you think the writer has done this?

_____

_____

1 mark

THE JURASSIC COAST

Test C - Year 5

Mary Anning was born in 1799 and raised in Lyme Regis in Dorset. She had no scientific training, but her special collection of fossils was of particular interest to scientists. For, at the time, very little was known about prehistoric animals.

Her parents were so poor, of the nine children they had, only two survived – Mary and her brother, Joseph. When she was eleven, her father died falling off a cliff, which made it even more important that Mary should find interesting pebbles and shells that visitors to the seaside might buy as souvenirs.

Although she was too poor to go to school, she was able to read and write, and was able to read about geology (how rocks are formed) and anatomy (how bodies work). She also drew many of the fossils she started to find on the beach. In prehistoric times, approximately 200 million years ago, Dorset was underneath the sea. As a result, there are many fossilised bones of creatures embedded in the rock and clay of the cliffs.

One day, when she and Joseph were searching for fossils, they discovered part of a crocodile-like skull sticking out of the rock. Carefully chipping away at the rock, they revealed the first complete skeleton of an ichthyosaurus. The word means *fish-lizard*.

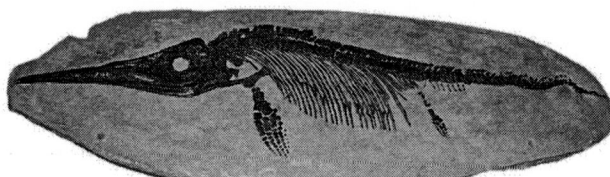

This created great excitement among scientists. Consequently, she became something of a celebrity. Professors of science wrote her letters and sent money to help her with her searches. She continued to successfully scour the beach for fossils and, unintentionally, helped to change what we know about life on Earth in prehistoric times. Soon, she was able to set up her own shop selling fossils to visitors. Nowadays, the Lyme Regis Museum is located on the spot where Mary Anning lived.

FOSSILIST'S GUIDE
The serious fossil hunter needs some important pieces of equipment. To remove possible fossils intact from rock, you will need a strong hammer and a chisel. To protect your eyes from flying rock splinters, safety glasses will prevent injury. A waterproof bag with strong straps and easily accessible pockets will be required for possible finds as well as sandwiches and a bottle of water. Sturdy walking boots will protect your ankles on uneven ground.
A final word of warning: NEVER ATTEMPT TO CLIMB THE CLIFFS.

Test C - Year 5

1. Describe **two** of the tragic events that happened in Mary's family as she was growing up.

   1) _____

   2) _____

   2 marks

2. How did the family try to make some extra money?

   _____

   1 mark

3. What kind of books were among those she read?

   _____

   1 mark

4. Why were scientists interested in her collection of fossils?

   _____

   _____

   1 mark

5. Why are there so many fossils to be found along the coast of Dorset?

   _____

   _____

   _____

   2 marks

© Copyright HeadStart Primary Ltd 2016

6. How did Mary Anning become a celebrity?

_____

_____

1 mark

7. How did life become better for her after the discovery of the ichthyosaurus fossil?

_____

1 mark

8. 'She continued to successfully scour the beach for fossils and, unintentionally, helped to change what we know about life on Earth in prehistoric times.'
What does **unintentionally** mean? **Circle one.**

| without meaning to | deliberately | without stress |

1 mark

9. Apart from finding your own fossils on the beach, where in Dorset do you think you might be able to see some fossils?

_____

1 mark

10. 'To extract possible fossils intact from rock...'
What does **intact** mean?
Circle one.

| hidden | sharp | complete |

1 mark

© Copyright HeadStart Primary Ltd 2016

Test C - Year 5

11. Write down **two** examples of equipment, suggested in the **Fossilist's Guide**, a serious fossil hunter would need in order to remove fossils from rocks.

   1) _____

   2) _____

   1 mark

12. Why do fossil hunters need to protect their eyes?

   _____

   _____

   1 mark

13. Why do fossil hunters need sturdy boots?

   _____

   _____

   1 mark

14. The last sentence in the FOSSILIST'S GUIDE is in bold. Why do you think that is?

   _____

   _____

   1 mark

© Copyright HeadStart Primary Ltd 2016

A Whale of a Tale

Test C - Year 5

Sunday 12th – last day of the holidays

Dear Diary,

    I must put this down on paper before the memory fades like the sea washing away a footprint in the sand.

    Despite the dark clouds, I went to the beach for the last time this morning. I watched a ship motionless on the horizon. I held a shell up to my ear. "Stay away, stay..." it seemed to whisper. Huh! My imagination!

    Then, down by the black rocks, I spotted something sticking half out of the sand. You couldn't miss it. A wonderful thing. A treasure. It looked exactly like the horn of a unicorn. Of course, it had to be a narwhal's tusk – one of those smaller Arctic whales. But this was treasure just the same.

    As I got closer the waves beat against the rocks like rolling thunder. Something told me the tusk wasn't mine to touch. I should leave it to take its chances with the tide.

    Brushing away the sand clinging to it, I couldn't believe my eyes. It was gold! As I struggled to dislodge it, the waves battered the rocks as if in a rage. The seagulls screeched and dived at me. I gave one last heave and fell backwards with the tusk in both hands. It was mine! But my back slammed hard against the sand. I felt dazed. Sick.

    Immediately, some mysterious force took me to the ship on the horizon – a whaleboat, surrounded by whales in a frenzy of anger. The engines were grinding, but no movement. The whale hunters, paralysed, stared straight ahead, trapped by some spell. "The giants of the deep," was all they mumbled.

    I don't know how I knew what to do, but I did. The crew looked even more terrified when I held up the narwhal tusk. Waves crashed high above the boat. Thunder cracked around our heads. I threw the golden tusk back, returning it to the sea.

    Then... what? Everything went calm. No boat. No crashing waves. I was lying on the beach, getting my breath back, wondering who to tell... and what to tell them.

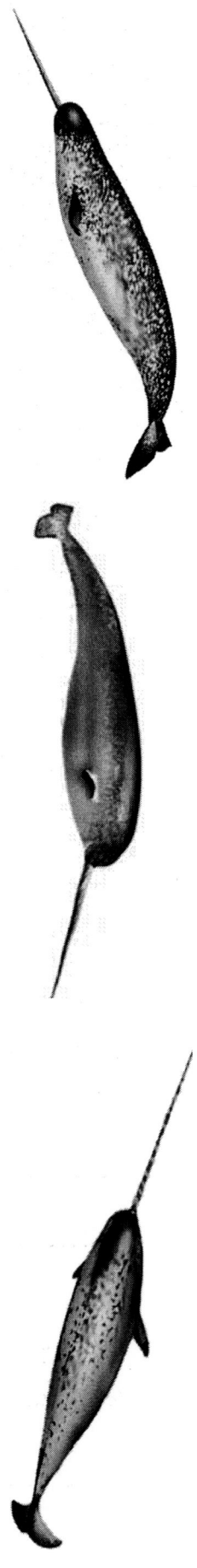

© Copyright HeadStart Primary Ltd 2016

Test C - Year 5

1. What is **like the sea washing away a footprint in the sand**?

   _____

   1 mark

2. This wasn't the writer's first visit to the beach. Write down the words that tell you.

   _____

   1 mark

3. The boat on the horizon is described as **motionless**. What does **motionless** mean? **Tick one.**

   without feelings ☐

   not moving ☐

   far away ☐

   1 mark

4. What does the writer not take seriously – as just **My imagination**?

   _____

   _____

   1 mark

5. Where on the beach was the narwhal tusk when the writer spotted it sticking out of the sand?

   _____

   1 mark

© Copyright HeadStart Primary Ltd 2016

6. The writer describes the tusk in **two ways** that suggest how special it appears to be. What are they?

   1) _____

   2) _____

   2 marks

7. What is the narwhal tusk similar to?

   _____

   1 mark

8. What do you think would happen to the tusk if it had been left to **take its chances with the tide**?

   _____

   _____

   1 mark

9. Look at the paragraph beginning: **I brushed away the sand...**
   Two things appear to be trying to protect the narwhal tusk. What are they?

   1) _____

   _____

   2) _____

   _____

   2 marks

10. How was the writer carried out to the whaleboat?

    _____

    1 mark

Test C - Year 5

11. Who or what are **the giants of the deep**?

    _____

    1 mark

12. What do you think happened to the crew of the whaleboat when the narwhal tusk was returned to the sea?

    _____

    _____

    _____

    2 marks

13. Why do you think the writer has written: **Then... what?**

    _____

    _____

    1 mark

14. Some words have been used in the diary that mean what they sound like. This is called onomatopoeia.
    Tick all three examples.

horizon	☐
screeched	☐
grinding	☐
cracked	☐
beach	☐

    2 marks

© Copyright HeadStart Primary Ltd 2016

Answers and Mark Scheme – Test C – Year 5

Secrets of the Woods

No.	Answers and Mark Scheme	Domain	Marks
1	at the top of trees / branches	2b	1
2	magical places / a world of mystery / explore its secrets **[Award 2 marks for any two correct answers; 1 mark for one correct answer.]**	2g	2
3	Squirrels can travel through the woods in safety high up in the trees.	2d	1
4	They receive more light.	2b	1
5	They sprawl sideways.	2b	1
6	insects – cracks and crevices in the bark of trees = 1 mark berries and nuts – bushes = 1 mark	2b	2
7	Flowers grow if they receive enough light.	2b	1
8	Holes in tree trunks provide nests for owls. = 1 mark Leaf litter provides nesting material. = 1 mark	2b	2
9	mosses / lichens / fungi /insects / other invertebrates **[Award 1 mark for any two correct answers.]**	2b	1
10	the roots stop the tree from blowing over	2a	1
11	It climbs up existing bushes and trees.	2b	1
12	It stops the soil being eroded.	2b	1
13	The arrows point to the parts of the picture referred to in the text. / The arrows help you to see which parts of the woodland the words in the boxes relate to. / The arrows link the information to the picture.	2e	1

© Copyright HeadStart Primary Ltd 2016

The Jurassic Coast			
No.	Answers and Mark Scheme	Domain	Marks
1	A number of her brothers and sisters died. = 1 mark Her father fell off a cliff. = 1 mark	2b	2
2	By selling interesting shells and pebbles to visitors.	2b	1
3	geology and anatomy / books on how rocks are formed and how the body works	2b	1
4	It provided them with evidence of prehistoric life on Earth.	2d	1
5	200 million years ago, Dorset was underneath the sea. = 1 mark Fossilised bones are embedded in the rock and clay of the cliffs. = 1 mark	2b	2
6	She (and her brother) discovered the first, complete ichthyosaurus skeleton. / Scientists were very excited by her discoveries.	2d	1
7	Scientists sent her money to help with her searches.	2d	1
8	without meaning to	2a	1
9	Lyme Regis Museum	2d	1
10	complete	2a	1
11	strong hammer / chisel / safety glasses / waterproof bag **[Award 1 mark for any two correct answers.]**	2b	1
12	When you are hammering, there is a danger of flying rock splinters going into your eyes.	2d	1
13	Fossilists need boots to protect their ankles on uneven ground.	2d	1
14	The words are in bold to draw the reader's attention to an important safety issue.	2e	1

© Copyright HeadStart Primary Ltd 2016

A Whale of a Tale			
No.	Answers and Mark Scheme	Domain	Marks
1	memory (fading)	2g	1
2	for the last time	2d	1
3	not moving	2a	1
4	The shell whispering: "Stay away, stay..."	2b	1
5	down by the black rocks	2b	1
6	A wonderful thing. = 1 mark A treasure. / But this was treasure just the same. = 1 mark [**Also accept:** It was gold!]	2b	2
7	horn of a unicorn	2b	1
8	It would be swept out to sea.	2d	1
9	The waves (battered the rocks as if in a rage). = 1 mark The seagulls (screeched and dived at me). = 1 mark	2b	2
10	some mysterious force	2b	1
11	whales	2d	1
12	They went back to steering the whaleboat / returned to harbour / were released from the spell. = 1 mark They vowed to stop hunting whales / had no memory of what happened and carried on as before. = 1 mark	2e	2
13	The writer was in a daze / couldn't explain what had happened, how the writer got back to the beach, or what would happen next.	2d	1
14	screeched, grinding, cracked [**Award 2 marks for three correct answers; 1 mark for two correct answers. Deduct 1 mark for each incorrect answer.**]	2g	2

	TOTAL	50

Tracking – using tests to track children's progress

Once a test has been marked, a score out of 50 can be awarded. This score should then be converted to a percentage.

The table below can then be used to identify progress against one of the 6 stages. The table uses percentage scores for conversion.

Year 5

Percentage Score	Stage	
0 – 25	Emerging	Less than expected progress
26 – 50	Developing	
51 – 63	Progressing	Expected progress
64 – 75	Secure	
76 – 88	Mastering	More than expected progress
89 – 100	Exceeding	

0 – 50%   Less than expected
51 – 75%   Expected
76 – 100% More than expected

PERRYMOUNT SCHOOL
SUNDERLAND ROAD
SE23 2PX
0208 699 4522
0208 291 9502

The assessments are intended to be used by teachers as a tool to support their professional judgement. The table above should be used only as a guide to achievement and progress. This data should always be used in conjunction with ongoing teacher assessment.